DO YOU BELIEVE
IN
MAGIC?

A WILD THING BOOK

DO YOU BELIEVE *IN* MAGIC?

BY

LAURA KRANTZ

A WILD THING BOOK

Abrams Books for Young Readers
New York

Cataloging-in-Publication Data has been applied for and may be
obtained from the Library of Congress.

ISBN 978-1-4197-5822-5

Text © 2024 Laura Krantz
Illustrations © 2024 Abrams
Edited by Howard W. Reeves
Illustrations and design by Rafael Nobre

Published in 2024 by Abrams Books for Young Readers, an imprint
of ABRAMS. All rights reserved. No portion of this book may be
reproduced, stored in a retrieval system, or transmitted in any form
or by any means, mechanical, electronic, photocopying, recording, or
otherwise, without written permission from the publisher.

Printed and bound in China
10 9 8 7 6 5 4 3 2

Abrams Books for Young Readers are available at special discounts
when purchased in quantity for premiums and promotions as well as
fundraising or educational use. Special editions can also be created to
specification. For details, contact specialsales@abramsbooks.com or
the address below.

Abrams® is a registered trademark of Harry N. Abrams, Inc.

ABRAMS The Art of Books
195 Broadway, New York, NY 10007
abramsbooks.com

To my sister, Ashley
And to Kira, Beth, and Alison,
for a lifetime of friendship

Any sufficiently advanced technology is indistinguishable from magic.
ARTHUR C. CLARKE

CONTENTS

I PUT A SPELL ON YOU

CRUNCH CRUNCH . . . CRUUUUUNCH CRUNCH CRUNCH . . . CRUNCH

Cassie Gibbs crushed several delicate dried eggshells into fragments in a small black stone bowl. The shells made a satisfying crunching noise as she pulverized them into jagged, bright-white bits. Once she'd ground them down to about the size of big snowflakes, she turned her attention to the other items laid out in front of her.

"That's our lavender. Then we're going to need cloves. And some orange peel," she said, listing off ingredients. Opening a jar, she tipped a few dozen cloves into another small bowl and added two dried orange peels. "Now a couple of cinnamon sticks. And salt." She poured a generous amount into another dish.

While it seemed like Cassie was whipping up some sort of odd dessert, she was actually showing me the items she uses to cast a spell. Yep—a spell! Specifically one that, if it worked, would summon a familiar. I wasn't entirely familiar (ha!) with what a familiar is, so I asked Cassie to explain.

"A familiar is some sort of spirit," Cassie told me. "It usually appears to us humans in animal form, but it's not always a pet. For example, some people constantly have crows following them around, or owls that show up wherever they go."

Cassie said that these spirits can aid and protect people who are practicing magic—people like her.

"I'm a witch," she explained. "I practice Celtic witchcraft—magic that comes from places like Scotland, Ireland, and Wales and has a lot to do with nature."

Now, when I hear the word witch, I usually think of the characters in the Harry Potter movies, or that book *The Witches* by my favorite author, Roald Dahl. Or I imagine someone with green skin standing over a steaming cauldron, wearing a big pointy hat, with a broomstick and a black cat nearby. Cassie did have a cat—a very friendly and curious calico with blue eyes named Esther (Esther, Cassie told me, was her familiar). But Cassie's skin was decidedly not green, and there was no hat or broomstick in sight.

At this point, you might be wondering why I was hanging out with a witch, especially one who crushed up eggshells and talked about familiars. Well, let me introduce myself. My name is Laura, and I'm a journalist. My job is to ask lots of questions and write about what I learn for other people to read. I like to write about the science of mysterious things, like Bigfoot and aliens, and for this book, I wanted to explore the world of magic because, well, it's also pretty mysterious. And what's more, sometimes even science seems a lot like magic. For instance, think about that magical device called a cell phone that lets you talk to someone on the other side of the country. Or how Earth is spinning at around one thousand miles per hour, but there's some sort of magical force that keeps us all from flying off into space. Or how a squirmy brown caterpillar magically changes into a beautiful butterfly.

I know there are good scientific explanations for all these things, but at first glance, they all look kind of magical. And to someone hundreds of years ago, they would have *definitely* seemed mysterious. That made me wonder about some of the other things we call magic, like spells and potions and super-stitions. Do those things work? Do they also have some science in them? That's part of what I wanted to find out. I decided to start by talking to people who practice casting spells or making potions or read-ing minds. While I didn't know anyone who did those things, a witch was

the first thing that popped into my head. A friend introduced me to Cassie, and she not only agreed to talk to me, but she even offered to create some sort of special spell to demonstrate how she practices magic.

After discussing several spell ideas—such as a spell to make your parents do what you want—we decided that it might be more fun to try to attract a familiar. As she mentioned earlier, Cassie's witchcraft involves nature and animals, so familiars were something she knew a lot about. Because the spell she had in mind was simple, without too many ingredients, she thought it would be a good one for someone like me, who didn't have a lot of magical experience.

You can imagine how curious I was by the time I arrived at Cassie's home on a stormy, early spring afternoon. In her living room, the shelves were stacked high with books about spells, witchcraft, and magic. Around us, candles blazed in a variety of glass containers, and smoke from a burning stick of incense wafted its spicy smell through the room. There were some sparkly quartz crystals and a few other colorful stones arranged in small dishes. But I didn't see any signs of a cauldron, and the ingredients for the spell she was casting were the kinds of things that many people have in their kitchens already, like salt and cinnamon.

Once she'd sorted out all the items she needed for the spell, Cassie gathered up her small ingredient bowls in a shallow dish and carried them, along with a tall white candle, to the altar in the corner of her living room. The altar, she told me, was her special spot for practicing her magic—in the same way that, if you were building something, you'd have a workbench. Cassie had made hers using a tree stump from the yard of the house she grew up in, and she'd covered it with two embroidered cloths—one dark purple with silver curlicues around the edges, and on top of that a smaller, light green cloth with gold thread. Cassie set the bowls down on the altar first, followed by the shallow dish and finally the candle.

Then she picked up a small brass bell and rang it delicately, signaling the start of the spell-casting ceremony. Taking a short, blunt dagger, she drew a circle in the air around the two of us and the altar and called to the four cardinal directions—east, south, west, and north—asking them to witness the spell.

As she finished this part of the ritual, Cassie placed the candle upright in the middle of the shallow dish. She began adding the other items one by one. The eggshells, she told me, were good for protection, as were the cloves and the salt. The orange peel would help with communication, and the lavender, she said, would help create a good relationship with the familiar. Finally, the cinnamon sticks added an element of love.

She lit the candle and then started speaking the words of the spell she'd written just for this:

I ask the universe to send me a special friend,
Bringing love that knows no beginning and no end.
Claw and tail and loving eyes,
Warm and gentle, wildly wise.
Let me know and let me see
A familiar here to do magic with me.

She uttered the words "So mote it be," which she said translated to "May it be so." We sat quietly on the floor of Cassie's living room for a few minutes, allowing the spell to take hold, and I thought about what kind of familiar I'd like to appear.

"It might be a pet you already have," she said softly after a few minutes. "But this familiar energy—this spirit energy—might join up with your pet, and it becomes more connected to you. Or maybe a new kitten will show up on your doorstep. Or birds start following you around."

I already had two very mischievous cats, and I didn't really want another pet. But having crows or owls flying around nearby whenever I'm outside sounded kind of cool. Or maybe hummingbirds? They're one of my favorite animals because they remind me of summer at my grandparents' cabin in Idaho. Once, I'd even had a baby hummingbird the size of a jellybean land on my finger! I knew I'd be watching pretty closely to see if any nearby animals started acting differently.

Then Cassie leaned forward to blow out the candle and declared our spell circle open. As wisps of smoke trailed upward, she told me to look for signs of a familiar showing up in the next few days.

"It's important to pay attention," she told me. Part of knowing if a spell has worked is being aware of what's going on around you and looking for signs, she explained. When she has cast familiar spells in the past, she has noticed more animals nearby—cats crossing her path, friends asking for help picking out a puppy—and it felt like something had responded to her spell.

Cassie didn't make any promises about this ceremony working. She said that even though we'd put our spell out into the world, it didn't mean a familiar would show up tomorrow—or ever. It could be that the timing is wrong for a familiar to appear, or that I would have to wait a good long while, maybe even years. But she seemed optimistic that something might happen.

I asked Cassie how she became interested in magic, and she told me that it had always been a huge part of her life and her family history. Two of her great-grandmothers were witches back in Scotland, and both her mother and her grandmother have had dreams that predicted the future. She started practicing magic when she was a teenager and then started teaching other people how to use magic, too. When I asked her how she describes magic to her students or to someone like me, who doesn't really know much about magic, she said she brings up the idea of energy.

"Energy affects everything around us," she explained. "We think about putting energy into something, and then that energy comes out as something else."

As an example, she pointed out that if you wanted to get an A on a test, you would put energy into studying and preparing. The end result of all that energy is that you know all the answers and do well.

"Spells kind of work the same way," she told me. "Today, we wanted to summon a familiar, so we gathered ingredients, prepared our spell, and put energy into that spell. And now we have to hope that the energy turns into the appearance of a familiar in our lives. It's like being a scientist. You experiment; you try to see what might happen."

I liked this idea about energy, and I was definitely curious about the possibility of a familiar. At the same time, I wasn't really sure that this spell would work, or how I would even know if it did. Doing a spell didn't seem like it was quite the same as doing a scientific experiment. How do you test magic? Is there any scientific proof of it? Does it match what we see in the movies?

Witches and spells and spirits, powerful beings that use special words and brew up potions—all this stuff was mysterious and fun to imagine, but I didn't know how it related to what I knew about science. Since I wanted to be honest with Cassie, I told her I wasn't so sure about all this.

"It's OK to have skepticism," she responded. "It's OK to say you're not one hundred percent on board. But I think it's worthwhile to be open-minded to all the different ideas of magic."

That seemed reasonable. I already thought there was a lot about science that seemed magical. Maybe there's more magic in everyday life than I realized, and I might find that science and magic have some things in common. Science might even explain some of the mysteries of magic. Those all seemed like some fairly good reasons to keep exploring this idea. I wasn't sure what I would find, but it was definitely time to start asking some questions.

SCIENCE VS. MAGIC

It had only been a couple of days since Cassie cast her spell, but so far I hadn't had much luck attracting a familiar. My two cats, Portia and Ichabod, were just running around, wrestling, and meowing as usual; I hadn't seen them doing anything different. No crows or owls had shown up when I went out for walks. I did see some very big and striped raccoons digging in my vegetable garden, but they certainly weren't helping (I think they ate my squash seeds!), so I doubted a raccoon was my new familiar. And I hadn't yet caught sight of any hummingbirds—it was probably still too cold. Maybe the spell hadn't worked? Or maybe it was just too soon to know? Cassie had told me that I shouldn't expect anything immediately—and that it could even be years!

While I was definitely holding out hope that Cassie's spell would work, deep down I wasn't sure it was possible. However, I'd promised Cassie I'd keep an open mind. And while I waited (very, very patiently) for a familiar to appear, I had the time to research different kinds of magic—and there are a lot of them! If I say the word *magic*, some people might immediately think of the Harry Potter books or the movie *Hocus Pocus*. Others might think of magic shows and magicians—pulling rabbits out of hats and sawing people in half. And still others might associate magic with people who claim to be able to predict the future or read minds. You might even have your own ideas about magic that are completely different from any of these.

Personally, I liked a definition of magic that I'd found in the dictionary: the ability to change events, get around the rules of nature, or otherwise control one's world through the use of mysterious forces. All the different types of magic I mentioned above fit pretty well into that definition. They're things that feel magical because, at first glance, we don't understand what's happening. There's some mystery there! But how realistic are they? I kept wondering if there was any science in those ideas. It's fun to imagine turning mice into horses or using a curse to cover the mean kid down the street in warts (just for a little while) or predicting the future with a crystal ball, but those things didn't seem possible. I really wanted to find examples of how magic and science might actually be related—and then I found one while reading a really interesting story about something called alchemy. Let me explain.

For hundreds of years, up until the 1700s, people tried to turn very common metals like lead or mercury into more rare and valuable metals like silver and gold. The name for this process was alchemy, and we called the people who did this kind of work alchemists. I've written lots more about this in chapter 3, but all you need to know right now is that, despite centuries of trying, the alchemists never succeeded in their goal. When people talk about alchemy now, they often dismiss it as silly, or they call it "magic," because turning lead into gold just doesn't seem possible.

Except that in 1941, a group of scientists at Harvard University in Massachusetts actually *did* turn mercury into gold. They used something called an atom smasher, which is exactly what its name sounds like—a machine that smashes tiny particles into atoms at astonishingly fast speeds to see how the atoms react.

In this case, the scientists used the machine to crash one small part of an atom—known as a neutron—into a mercury atom. This changed the structure of the mercury atom, and turned it into an atom of gold. Pretty amazing, right? Now, this was a different kind of gold than you might find in jewelry. For one, it was very radioactive, which meant it was dangerous to humans. Additionally, creating this kind of gold required very special, very expensive equipment, plus a tremendous amount of energy to power that equipment. And the process didn't make very much gold—no one was going to get rich from this experiment. In fact, it cost way more to make the gold than the gold was actually worth. But the scientists did turn one type of metal into another, which was the alchemists' dream.

Hmm, I thought after reading this story. ***Sounds like alchemy wasn't such a silly idea after all. Maybe they just didn't have the right tools at that time . . .***

As I read more about it, I found out that, even though the alchemists never succeeded at turning lead into gold, a lot of what they learned eventually became the foundation of the science of chemistry—the study of what everything is made of and how those things interact. Basically, the "magical" idea of alchemy played an important part in science and how we understand the world today. And alchemy wasn't the only example I came across of how the worlds of science and magic intersect. There were examples not only in chemistry but also botany (the study of plants) and astronomy (the study of the universe).

Take potions, for example. When I thought of magic potions, I thought of foul-smelling, fizzy liquids that could bring someone love or luck. Or some sort of strange witch's brew—a bubbling concoction of herbs and powders with the power to stop a fever or cure a headache. Actually, now that I think about it, that last example doesn't seem all that strange. After all, I drank down a pretty gross red goop the last time I had a cold, and it made me feel better. Only I didn't call it a potion; I just called it medicine, and it turns out that some of the key ingredients in it come from plants that are known for their healing properties. Maybe there is something scientific about potions.

Basically, as I read more information and talked to more people, I learned that some of the things I'd thought of as magic really are part of my everyday life. There's even the possibility that *you* might be using magic, even if you don't realize it. Do you try to avoid stepping on cracks or walking under ladders? Or maybe you carry a lucky object with you? Do you ever drink ginger ale when you don't feel well? All of those actions could be seen as magical, *and* they might have something scientific about them!

I knew if I was really going to explore this world, I needed to approach it in a logical manner and see what actually made sense. But how would I figure out if a magical practice had something scientific about it? Cassie had said that she likes to experiment with magic, so maybe I could set up an experiment of my own to test out different magics. After all, that's how science works. Scientists use experiments and observations to learn more about the world. If they have a question, they'll come up with a hypothesis for what the possible answer might be. You've probably learned about the scientific method and constructed your own hypotheses in school, or even outside of school. In case you haven't (or you need a refresher): A hypothesis is the scientists' best guess, based on the information they already know is true. Then they'll test that hypothesis with an experiment—do the results of that experiment support or contradict their hypothesis? The process scientists use to answer questions is known as the scientific method. It's a set of directions for trying to explain something, and there are six basic steps:

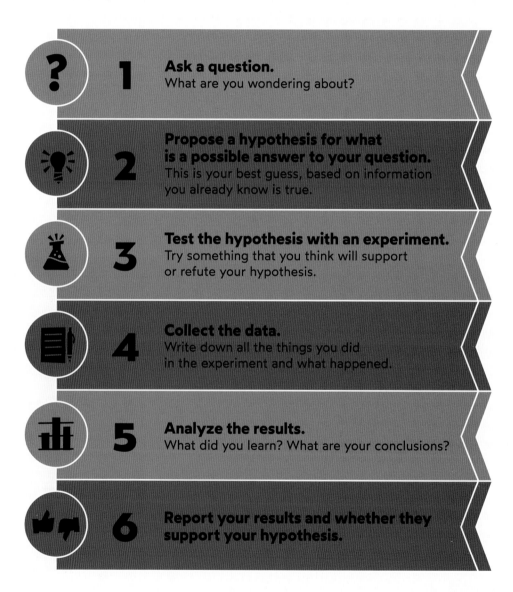

1 Ask a question.
What are you wondering about?

2 Propose a hypothesis for what is a possible answer to your question.
This is your best guess, based on information you already know is true.

3 Test the hypothesis with an experiment.
Try something that you think will support or refute your hypothesis.

4 Collect the data.
Write down all the things you did in the experiment and what happened.

5 Analyze the results.
What did you learn? What are your conclusions?

6 Report your results and whether they support your hypothesis.

It's important that scientists don't let their feelings get in the way. Science is supposed to be objective, which means that it's only about facts, not feelings or beliefs. After all, scientists are humans just like the rest of us. They might hope for a certain answer to their question, but they have to put those hopes aside and pay attention to what their experiment actually shows.

If the experiment didn't support their hypothesis, then the scientists will propose a different one and repeat all the steps. This is called iteration. Think of making a paper airplane—if it doesn't fly the first time, you'll keep adjusting your design until it does. Those tweaks are iterations. But often, even if an experiment *does* support the hypothesis, a scientist will test it over and over again to see if they keep getting the same result. Other scientists will probably test the hypothesis, too, using the same experiments. Only if all the scientists keep getting the same answer do they know that the hypothesis is right.

That method seems like a good way to start, I thought. *I'll try to come up with an experiment about magic.*

I wasn't so sure how to do this, though. How could I use the scientific method to test whether something that seems magic is real? I spoke with Dr. Chris Gosden, who told me that—unfortunately— magic can't be tested using those same rules. Dr. Gosden is an archaeologist, a type of scientist who studies people and the things they made and left behind long ago. He's spent time studying magical practices, and he wrote a book about the history of magic—from thousands and thousands of years ago up to the present day.

"In science, there are things that we think wouldn't work," he explained. "Things like saying words that we might call spells, or writing something on a piece of paper that might be a curse, or killing a chicken in a special way."

Or casting a spell to attract a familiar? I wondered.

"But," he went on, "if you believe in magic, you think these types of actions *will* have an effect. You believe that your actions *can* influence the world around you."

Basically, he told me that science is about standing back and observing and collecting information through the rules set out by the scientific method—it's supposed to be objective. Magic, on the other hand, could be considered **subjective**, because it's based on personal feelings and belief rather than facts.

Here's an example of subjectivity: Let's say I have a bowl with exactly sixty-five peanut M&Ms in it. We can count the M&Ms, and we can all agree that there are sixty-five candies. That makes the number of M&Ms a fact, so it is **objective**. But if I say that, out of those sixty-five candies, the orange ones are the best, we might not all agree on that. You might think the red or blue ones are better. Our feelings about which color is best are subjective—there's no way to say which color is best, because it's based on personal preference, not facts. The scientific method would work for the question "How many M&Ms are in that bowl?" But it wouldn't work for the question "What color M&M is the best?"

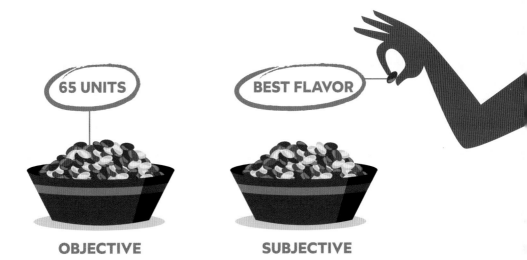

As I thought about the scientific method in terms of magic, I could see why it would be hard to do an experiment. Just thinking about the spell I did with Cassie: What if an animal doesn't show up until years later—could I say it was because of the spell? Or is it just chance? Are there *any* time limits? It seems like it would be hard to do an experiment if a spell could last forever. And how would I prove that an animal showed up because of the spell and not for some other reason—like raiding my vegetable garden?

I'd been defining magic as the idea that humans can use mysterious forces to control the world around them. But if something mysterious does happen, would we know if it was magic? Or if there is perhaps something else going on? And can a person be both scientific *and* believe in magic? I clearly had a lot more to learn about this topic. While I probably couldn't use traditional scientific experiments to investigate magic, I could still be careful about verifying facts and making sure the information I found was logical before I shared it. And I knew I'd need to be objective—I had to look at the facts without letting my personal feelings and skepticism get in the way. All of this was part of being a good journalist—along with asking questions.

Coming up with those questions wouldn't be too hard, though—I already had a *lot*. I wanted to know more about the kinds of magical practices that I'd heard people actually do in the real world (as opposed to just in books and movies), such as alchemy, potions, curses, and superstitions. That meant talking to scientists, witches, magicians, and other experts to hear their thoughts.

And I was super curious about the history of magic. Where did our idea of witches first come from? When did people start using curses? Or come up with the idea that the stars might be able to predict the future? What made people decide that magic and science were two very different things? I figured that a good place to start with all these questions would be by looking into the past, because—as Dr. Gosden pointed out—we humans have been thinking about magic for thousands and thousands and thousands of years.

A (BRIEF) MAGICAL HISTORY

Why do people use magic? And when did we start? And did people in the past think about magic the same way we do today? When I started reading about the history of magic, I realized that it's been part of human life perhaps forever. It traces pretty far back—like tens of thousands of years, possibly even longer—and a lot of those ancient magical practices explain some of the beliefs that people have now. But I knew there was absolutely no way I'd be able to write about all that history in just one chapter, not unless I used some sort of magic shrinking spell.

I decided to hopscotch through history a bit, learning about different magical practices like astrology and hunting magic, and also some of the times and places that seemed to play a big part in shaping many of our current ideas about magic, like Ancient Egypt and Greece. And I especially wanted to see what types of magic might have some relationship with science.

So when did humans start practicing magic? It's not entirely clear. Archeologists and anthropologists—the scientists who study humans, both past and present—think that people have always had magical practices as a way of trying to understand, and have some control over, the big and sometimes scary world around them. That fit pretty well with the definition I'd been using: that magic is the ability to change events or control the world using supposedly mysterious forces. And people have used magic everywhere—in India, China, Japan, England, Australia, Peru, Greenland, Congo, Canada, and anywhere else you can think of (although probably not Antarctica)—even before any of those countries existed.

We humans—what scientists call *Homo sapiens*—have been around for at least two hundred thousand years. There is a lot that archaeologists don't know about those earliest humans. Hundreds of thousands of years ago, the world would have looked very different from the world we know today, with all kinds of animals and plants we've never seen, and strange sights and smells. Plus, humans then may not have spoken any language, and they certainly didn't have our modern technologies like the internet (or toilet paper), so their lives looked very different from ours. Scientists have found bones and ancient stone tools, so they're certain that humans back then hunted animals and gathered plants for food. Not much else remains of our early ancestors, though, which means there's really no way to know what the people who lived back then were thinking or what they believed.

But about fifty thousand years ago, during a time period known as the Upper Paleolithic, humans began to invent and create things that remained long after the people who made them had died. These ancient items called artifacts stuck around—in caves, or at old campsites—where archaeologists found them and got a better sense of what our ancestors' lives might have been like. Among these artifacts were tools like arrowheads and spear points, as well as knife blades. Even cooler? The archaeologists also found examples of art in the form of cave paintings and carvings of animals.

These cave paintings show up in lots of places, from Indonesia to Mongolia to Europe. They depict all kinds of different animals, including reindeer, camels, ostriches, and saber-toothed cats. There are also drawings of strange half-human, half-animal beasts that don't resemble any real creatures (that we know of . . .). Archaeologists don't know exactly why our ancestors created such artwork, but one possibility is that ancient humans used this art to make sure a hunt would be successful, a practice that some archaeologists call "hunting magic." The belief is that by drawing the animals, humans would then have some sort of mysterious power over the animals and be able to catch them. And our ancestors didn't just draw these animals—they also made carvings.

"There's a mammoth's tusk from a cave in Germany called Hohlenstein-Stadel," said Dr. Gosden, the anthropologist we met in the last chapter who wrote a book on the history of magic. "It was carved into a figure with the head of a lion and the body of a human. Of course, we don't know at all why they did this, but it could be they were trying to create a magical combination of the strengths of the mammoth, the lion, and the human into one object."

Was it used for a hunting spell? I wondered. *Or was it just a carving of something you don't want to run into on a dark night in the forest?* Either way, it certainly seemed magical.

You might be wondering—because I sure did—how do we know that this art was used for magic, and not just because people liked drawing animals? We don't. That's part of the mystery, and it's something scientists might not ever know for sure. As Dr. Gosden put it, "The past is a foreign country, and the way we understand the world now is very different from fifty thousand years ago."

We can't know what people back then were thinking. But even if some of what they drew and created seemed fantastical, those creations were likely part of how people thought the world worked. And based on some of the artifacts they've found, scientists are pretty sure people back then were observing everything around them and making note of all the animals and plants, along with the weather and the sky.

"Archaeologists in Europe found a limestone staff made of mammoth ivory," Dr. Gosden told me. "It's about twenty thousand years old and has a whole series of marks on it that could have something to do with the cycles of the moon. Again, we don't know for sure, but it could well be that people were observing the moon and making notes of how it changed." That seemed almost scientific to me! Even if those early humans didn't have the understanding of the moon that we do now, they appeared to be trying to figure it out.

If artifacts helped scientists understand how our ancestors thought about the world, actual written words were even more important. The oldest known writing comes from about 5,500 years ago. It's actually a pictogram, meaning it uses pictures to symbolize words (today, emojis are a type of pictogram), although scientists haven't yet deciphered what this ancient writing means. The first pictographs came from Mesopotamia, where Iraq and parts of Iran, Kuwait, Turkey, and Syria are now. Around the same time, writing also appeared in Ancient Egypt—hieroglyphs, like those you might have seen in photos or in museums. Dr. Gosden explained to me why this was so exciting for archaeologists.

"The great thing about Egypt and Mesopotamia, compared with the Paleolithic, is that we have written texts. We can read what people wrote down and actually *know* that they were interested in the sun, the moon, and the stars."

They would have seen the predictable sunrises and sunsets. They would have followed the phases of the moon, from big fat full moons to slivered crescents to no moon at all. They would have noticed how the stars moved across the sky. And then there were events that would have been surprising—things like comets, that only pass through the sky every few hundred years. Imagine not knowing anything about comets—or that they even existed—and then seeing one flame through the heavens! How would you even explain that? Magic, maybe?

It's not surprising that people back then might not have understood what the moon was or why it moved the way it did or why it sometimes disappeared. However, like those early Paleolithic humans, the Egyptians and Mesopotamians also saw that it followed a regular pattern, and they came up with their own ways of tracking it, along with stories about why it did what it did.

In addition, they created a detailed system for understanding what effect the movement of all those heavenly bodies would have on a human's life. This system is known as astrology, and the people who study it are called astrologers. Astrology is based on the idea that the movement of planets and stars can predict the future and that where the stars are in the sky when you're born will determine things about your life, like certain personality traits. It's something that many people still believe in. You might have even heard a friend say something like "I'm a Scorpio."

THE ZODIAC

The zodiac is a belt of space that surrounds Earth. It's defined by the area where the sun appears to move around Earth over an entire year. Of course, Earth moves around the sun, but the people who came up with the idea of the zodiac—roughly two thousand years ago—didn't know that yet. They believed that Earth was at the center of our solar system.

In this band of space, there are twelve constellations—groups of stars—that make up the signs of the Western zodiac. Each one takes up one-twelfth of that circle around our planet. From here on Earth, those clusters of stars look like certain shapes or creatures, which is how the constellations got their names. Since a lot of the constellations are named after animals, the ancient Greeks called this belt the zodiakos kyklos—the circle of animals.The Greeks weren't the first to come up with the idea of the zodiac—that was probably the Mesopotamians.

But the Greek version of the zodiac has barely changed in 2,000 years and would look pretty famiilar to a Greek time traveler from the year 100!

Your astrological sign is based on where the Sun is located in the zodiac when you're born. As Earth rotates, different constellations are more visible in the night sky during certain times of the year. In fact, it's whatever part of the circle *can't* be seen when someone is born—because the constellation is out during the day and not at night—that determines their astrological sign.

Here are the twelve constellations of the zodiac and the dates that early astrologers noticed lined up with each sign:

 AQUARIUS
THE WATER BEARER
(JANUARY 20–FEBRUARY 18)

 PISCES,
THE FISH
(FEBRUARY 19–MARCH 20)

 ARIES
THE RAM
(MARCH 21–APRIL 19)

 TAURUS
THE BULL
(APRIL 20–MAY 20)

 GEMINI
THE TWINS
(MAY 21–JUNE 21)

 CANCER
THE CRAB
(JUNE 22–JULY 22)

 LEO
THE LION
(JULY 23–AUGUST 22)

 VIRGO
THE VIRGIN
(AUGUST 23–SEPTEMBER 22)

 LIBRA
THE SCALES
(SEPTEMBER 23–OCTOBER 23)

 SCORPIO
THE SCORPION
(OCTOBER 24–NOVEMBER 21)

 SAGITTARIUS
THE ARCHER
(NOVEMBER 22–DECEMBER 21)

 CAPRICORN
THE GOAT
(DECEMBER 22–JANUARY 19)

> Astrologers assigned these dates to each constellation a long, long time ago, based on their observations of the night sky. However, over the years, the angle at which Earth rotates has shifted, so while these same dates are still used, they don't necessarily line up to the same constellation anymore. For example, if you were born on January 1, you would actually be a Sagittarius now, instead of a Capricorn.
>
> Other cultures also have zodiac systems. The Hindu zodiac, used in India, may be partially based on the Greek one. The Chinese zodiac—which has variations all over Asia—also has twelve signs, but they are not based on constellations.

It's important to note that astrology is very different from astronomy. While astronomy is a recognized branch of science that deals with the study of the universe and everything in it—like planets, galaxies, moons, and asteroids—many modern scientists consider astrology to be magical and unscientific, especially when people claim it can be used to make predictions. Modern-day astrologers say that they can forecast the future based on the movement of the stars and planets, but scientists have tested those claims and found that the astrologers' predictions were no more accurate than those of someone who was just randomly guessing. And scientists also haven't seen any proof that stars affect people's lives, like determining whom you marry or if you'll be a good athlete.

But even so, astrology can't be ignored entirely. We know that for over four thousand years—from about 3000 BCE up until the 1600s—people treated astrology as a science. They used math to make accurate calculations about what they saw in the sky. They asked questions.

And they tried to come up with good answers, based on their observations and the knowledge they had at the time.

"All these societies that used what we now would call 'magical practices' also had scientific knowledge, even if they might not have called it that," said Dr. Gosden. Once people's scientific knowledge improved and they realized that the sun was at the center of the solar system—and all the planets, including Earth, were moving around it—they understood that astrology wasn't correct. But it's important to remember that much of what astrologers learned became the foundation for the science of astronomy. We didn't get to the science until we experimented with the magic.

Dr. Gosden pointed out that this was also true with medicine. Both Egyptian and Mesopotamian societies had elaborate rituals and magical practices to deal with health and illness. The Mesopotamians had several types of professional magic healers, who each had a long list of all the things they needed to know in order to do their job, such as specific rituals for opening temples, spells to protect against demons, and all kinds of ways to cure people of their health problems.

A (BRIEF) MAGICAL HISTORY • **33**

The Mesopotamians believed that demons caused a lot of illnesses—for instance, toothaches were supposedly caused by tooth worms, and to get rid of them, the healer would recite a special chant and then either use herbs to heal the tooth or simply pull it out of the patient's mouth. Anti-demon spells seem pretty magical, but the healers also clearly knew more practical ways to make people feel better.

The Egyptians had their own magical healing practices. Archaeologists found a papyrus from about 1500 BCE with all kinds of medical information in it, like how to deal with a parasite known as the guinea worm and how the heart works, along with what kinds of spells to say over a patient. Like the Mesopotamians, scientists think that Egyptian healers would have used both magic and herbs to cure people. For instance, if someone had a fish bone stuck in their throat, the healer would make a cake, say a spell over it, and then tell the patient to eat it (which might have helped to dislodge the bone). Or if someone got a cut, the healer would have used a magic spell, and also put a potion made of honey and special salts on the cut. We'll hear more about this in a later chapter, but some of these potions would have been very effective, even if the healers didn't always understand *why* they worked.

It's not surprising that the Mesopotamians and the Egyptians had some similar ideas. Dr. Gosden pointed out that magical practices didn't just stay in one place. As empires rose and fell and people traveled to other countries, these ideas would spread from one place to the next—like from Ancient Egypt to Ancient Greece. The Greeks were very interested in all kinds of magic. They believed certain stones had magical powers that could help them get rid of the stomach flu or protect them if they had to make a long trip. Magicians in Ancient

Greece had amulets—objects they claimed had special powers that could protect the wearer or bring them good luck—and they used all kinds of potions, which they called pharmaka.

Pharmaka! I thought. ***That sounds an awful lot like the word pharmacy . . .***

The Greeks—and later the Romans—also used curses. Archaeologists have found items known as curse tablets from as early as 600 BCE. They're not big stone tablets but rather very thin sheets of lead rolled up with pieces of pottery, papyrus, and sometimes gemstones, all inscribed with bits of writing. Scientists excavating ancient ruins have found these tablets buried alongside little figurines made of wax, clay, or wool. A Greek or Roman person who wanted to curse someone could use one of these tablets for any reason. Maybe they wanted a rival to lose a chariot race, or maybe someone else stole their crush, or perhaps someone took their clothes from the local bathhouse! The person performing the curse would wrap or attach a small figurine—along with some human hair from the person being cursed, or a bundle of magic herbs—to one of these tablets. Sometimes they'd pierce it with a nail. And then they'd throw the tablet into a special pit or a body of water or even bury it in a grave.

The Greeks also used a magical practice known as *divination*, which is predicting or foretelling the future (astrology is a type of divination). If someone wanted to know what the future would bring, they could go to an oracle—a priest or priestess who spoke on behalf of the gods—and ask a question or seek advice. The most famous of these was the Oracle at Delphi. People came to the oracle from Greece and beyond for answers to all sorts of questions, like when to plant a crop or get married or declare war. The Oracle at Delphi—who was always a woman—was said to communicate with the gods on their behalf and then provide an answer.

Divination didn't just happen in Greece—it appeared in many cultures throughout centuries. The Chinese began using divination at least as far back as four thousand years ago. They didn't have oracles, but a person with a question could go to a diviner, who would hear the question and then place a bone or a tortoise shell in a fire, causing it to crack. The diviner interpreted those cracks and looked for patterns that would supply an answer to the question. What was awesome for archaeologists is that someone would always carve both the question and the answer into the bone, so when scientists found those remains, they could tell what people were thinking. Other forms of divination involved something called cleromancy. The diviner would throw a collection of bones, shells, stones, or grass stalks onto the ground and interpret the resulting patterns. This wasn't just in China, but also in Europe, Africa, the Americas, and all over the world, and some people still use this practice.

TAROT CARDS

While there are lots of types of divination, the one that many people are most familiar with is known as *cartomancy*. This type of fortune telling uses a deck of cards, and the most famous version is known as tarot.

Initially, tarot had nothing to do with telling fortunes. The cards were originally created in Italy in the fifteenth century to play games. To play tarot, players added a pack of twenty-two special cards, known as triumph cards, to a deck of fifty-six traditional playing cards. There were four suits: wands, coins, cups, and swords (similar to the spades, hearts, diamonds, and clubs of modern playing cards). And there were fourteen cards in each suit: ten numbered cards and then a king, queen, knight, and jack. The triumph cards had beautiful artwork on them that represented animals, people, or natural forces like the moon. In total, a tarot deck has seventy-eight cards, and people played different variations of the game all over Europe.

However, in the eighteenth century, a Frenchman by the name of Antoine Court de Gébelin claimed that the cards actually contained special information from the old Egyptian gods. De Gébelin said the artwork on the triumph cards symbolized this secret knowledge (known as *arcana* in Latin) and that it could be used to predict the future. Other people began to make similar claims, and eventually fortune tellers divided the tarot deck into two parts—the minor arcana, which were the normal playing cards, and the major arcana, which were the triumph cards.

If you had a question about your life, you would pay a visit to a cartomancer, who would have you shuffle the deck. The fortune teller would then choose a few cards to lay face up and determine the answer to your question based on what cards appeared, whether they faced you or the fortune teller, and what cards appeared alongside them.

There is zero evidence that the cards have anything to do with Ancient Egypt—or that they can predict the future—but even today, people are fascinated by the idea of having their cards "read" to help solve a problem or to see what fate has in store for them.

Today, we might not consult the Oracle at Delphi, but we still try to predict the future so we can be better prepared. Meteorologists try to predict the weather. Doctors try to predict how tall you'll be when you grow up, or if you might develop a certain disease. Farmers try to predict what crops to plant and when. The tools we have now for making those predictions are probably more exact than the Oracle at Delphi—but we still don't have all the answers and there's always an element of chance.

As you can see from all these examples—and believe me, there are *lots* more—magic was everywhere, in all cultures, all the way back in human history. And what I noticed is that certain practices—alchemy, astrology, potions, curses, divination—appear in different places and at different times over and over and over again. I asked Dr. Gosden

why he thought these particular ideas caught on, and even more importantly, why humans use magic at all.

"I think that people use magic to try to answer big questions," he replied. "Things like, how do you make sure kids are born safely? How do you grow up healthy? What happens after you die? How do you make someone you don't like get sick? Magic is about the big issues of life and death, and those are issues that people have everywhere, throughout history."

Ultimately, as Dr. Gosden pointed out, people wanted to have answers for those big life questions because they wanted to feel like they had a little bit of control. Control helps us feel more powerful in the face of uncertainty or big forces. And if you're just a human in a big, empty landscape with saber-toothed cats and volcanoes, having a sense of control—of an ability to *do* something—is no small thing. Or if you're living in the sixth century and you want to make sure your crop turns out well or that your baby is born healthy, these methods might allow you to feel like you are taking action to make that happen.

Aha! I thought. ***Using mysterious forces to change the outcome of something.***

"So what happened?" I asked Dr. Gosden. "If these kinds of magical practices were something that so many people believed in for so long, when did that change?"

Well, he told me, magic really got pushed aside during the Middle Ages, around the year 500 CE. At that time, important religious figures began claiming that magic was bad, used by evil sorcerers and witches. In places like China or the Middle East, you could be punished for using magic to harm people. But in Europe, you could be punished for using any kind of magic at all! European church leaders, kings, and emperors declared that using magic was a sin and that anyone caught practicing it would be punished. In 789 CE, Emperor Charlemagne went so far as to condemn all sorcerers to death. Because of this, people started to view magic in a more negative light. They grew suspicious and fearful of anyone who claimed to have magical abilities. It was a pretty dangerous time to be associated with anything magical. Someone like Cassie could have gotten in a lot of trouble back then!

Some people did continue to practice magic and still created spells, cursed their enemies, or tried to bring about good fortune for themselves and people they trusted. Other people secretly visited practitioners of magic who would tell them the future by reading their palms, interpreting their dreams, or using numerology (a belief that certain numbers are important, like "lucky" numbers). And of course there were herbalists and healers creating potions and tonics. But even those gathering plants for medicinal use had to be careful—if someone afraid of magic saw what they were doing, those healers could be accused of witchcraft and arrested.

Magic, which had once been pretty common in people's lives, was now hidden away or completely avoided. That changed a little during the Renaissance, when artists, inventors, and thinkers—people like Leonardo da Vinci—wondered if magic could maybe answer the questions they had. These Renaissance thinkers brought back magical practices like alchemy and astrology to see if those ideas could help explain the natural world. But it was a short revival—by the 1700s, we were in a period of time known as the Enlightenment.

Scientists had puzzled out some of the questions that had been mysteries for all of human existence—things like the laws of physics, such as gravity. They knew that Earth moved around the sun. They understood medicine better, although I still wouldn't have wanted to see a doctor back then—they didn't yet understand germs, so no one washed their hands before operating on patients! Now that scientists had all this new knowledge, the old beliefs—the magical beliefs—seemed backward and superstitious in comparison. Where magic had once explained everything, Dr. Gosden said, now we had science to explain it.

"People tried to create a dividing line between science and magic," he told me. "Starting in the eighteenth century, we started to say, 'We're going to call these things over here science, and we're going to call these other things magic.'"

I understood why the scientists of the 1700s and later might look back and think that earlier ideas about demons and curses were silly or superstitious (such as the idea that demons, not bacteria, caused toothaches). But it did seem to me, based on what I'd learned so far, that the scientists and doctors in the Enlightenment weren't all that different from the sorcerers, witches, and astrologers of long ago. They had questions about the world. They looked for patterns and made observations about nature and other humans. They used what they learned to come up with their hypotheses about the world, how it worked, and, sometimes, how they could make events work in their favor. From that perspective, magic and science definitely seem to have some things in common.

I also found it interesting that magical practices were handed down from generation to generation and from culture to culture. People would try new things, and as they did, they would end up inventing a new way to do alchemy or a more precise way of observing stars and planets. Back then, knowledge was constantly changing and evolving, the same way it does today when we gather new information through scientific experimentation or develop new technology. As we've learned more about physics and chemistry and biology, and as our tools have gotten better, we dismiss those earlier ways of looking at the world by calling them "magic." Yet many of the things people did back then were the first steps toward our modern sciences.

There's one other thing to remember: We're always learning. There are a lot of things that scientists still don't understand. The science of today is great, but it doesn't pretend to have all the answers. We simply make our best guesses—our hypotheses—about how things work, based on what we've seen, and just like the people who came before us, we could be totally wrong. It could be that thousands of years from now, future people—with their new technologies and better understanding of the world—will look back at us and wonder what kinds of magical, superstitious things we were thinking!

FROM LEAD INTO GOLD

If I could have any magical power (other than attracting a familiar . . .), I think I'd like one that allowed me to turn one kind of object into another. I mean, I know I can turn a bowl of goo into a cake, or liquid water into solid ice. But I'm talking about transforming dogs into cats, spinach into lasagna, or plastic bottles into fresh flowers. And while *those* don't really seem possible, I'm not the only one who's dreamed of having this kind of power. In fact, for a very long time, people thought they could make at least one major transformation: turning lead into gold. Which would be a pretty amazing ability, right? If you could turn a super common type of metal into one that was very rare and valuable . . . well, you'd never have to worry about money.

Archaeologists know that alchemists started pursuing this dream at least two thousand years ago, because they've found written records of it. But humans had been working with metals well before then, so it's probably fair to guess that our ancestors had been trying to make one kind of metal out of another long before we started writing those ideas down.

And, as we learned in the first chapter, alchemy was one of the magical arts that appeared all over the world: Greece, China, India, the Middle East, and finally in Europe. I mean, I can see why it was such a popular idea. Who wouldn't want to turn lead into gold? But what made people think this was even possible? To find out, I called Dr. Lawrence Principe, who teaches both chemistry and the history of science; he's even written a book about alchemy. Dr. Principe told me that part of the reason people believed alchemy would work was because, once upon a time, they had a very different view of the world.

Starting in Ancient Greece, there was a theory that the whole world was evolving, from less perfect to more perfect. The people who came up with this idea were known as philosophers—they studied nature and looked for truth and knowledge in order to understand what it meant to be human. They believed that metals in the earth matured or evolved over time because of underground water and heat and that they would eventually become purified. For instance, they considered something like lead to be a very imperfect type of metal, while shiny gold was a perfect one.

"This was actually based on observations," Dr. Principe told me. "Every miner knew that the bits of silver he was digging out of the ground contained a lot of lead—they were never far apart from one another.

And silver ores always contained some gold, as if one metal was turning into another."

The Greek philosophers thought that, over a long period of time, lead would become silver and then eventually gold. Rather than wait the thousands of years that they thought it would take for this to happen, the Greeks wanted to find some sort of shortcut to speed everything up—a process known as alchemy.

Now, the Ancient Greek idea of what the world was made of was very different from what we know today. The beliefs of one philosopher by the name of Aristotle became very popular. He thought that everything in the world was made up of something called prime matter (or first matter) and was some combination of four basic elements: water, air, fire, and earth. Those four elements each had two of four specific qualities: hot, cold, dry, and wet. So water was cold and wet; air was hot and wet; fire was hot and dry; and earth was cold and dry.

In the Greeks' view of the world, everything was made up of some mix of those four elements. Here's an example I found about wood: Since wood burns, it contains fire. As it burns, it gives off smoke and releases steam, so it also contains air and water. When it finishes burning, the wood is reduced to ashes, which look like dirt, so it contains earth. The Greeks had a hypothesis that, by changing the exact mixture of elements, they could change one object into another. For example, if you heat up wet, soft clay (earth) in an oven, you're reducing the amount of water and you're adding fire and hot air, turning the clay into a different kind of earth.

I got how the Greeks came up with this idea. It wasn't a bad way of trying to understand how nature worked. But where setting sticks on fire and making clay harden are easy, turning lead into gold was much more difficult. Aristotle thought that it might require some sort of not-yet-discovered *fifth* element—a substance that was the most evolved, most pure element ever to exist. By adding a piece of this element to something like lead, you'd be able to speed up nature and change it into gold immediately. But what was that element? No one knew for sure.

CHINESE ALCHEMY

Alchemy in China differed from alchemy in Ancient Greece and later in the Middle East and Europe. The Chinese philosophers believed there were five elements—earth, metal, water, wood, and fire. Similar to other alchemists, they wanted to figure out how to transform metals, but for them, it was less about getting wealthy and more about creating elixirs (or potions) that would make them healthier. In fact, Chinese alchemists hoped they might be able to use alchemy to create a tonic—a sort of medicine—that would let them live forever.

They mixed up all kinds of liquids they thought might do the trick, but there was a real problem: This kind of medicine was poisoning people. Many of the substances that Chinese alchemists put in their elixirs were actually quite deadly. Mercury and arsenic—two of the ingredients that they used—are not meant to be swallowed or eaten. After drinking some sort of concoction that was supposed to give them eternal life, at least six Chinese emperors died.

While the alchemists in China didn't manage to bring about everlasting life, their experiments did lead to at least one very important discovery—gunpowder. Gunpowder is made from three main ingredients: sulfur, charcoal, and a chemical compound called potassium nitrate or saltpeter. Do not try making this at home. Why?

In the ninth century, when alchemists combined these three items to make their elixirs, they realized very quickly that the mixture would erupt in flames and sometimes explode. The people doing these experiments made notes to warn other alchemists of the danger. They gave this combination a name that, translated into English, means "fire medicine."

It wasn't very useful as an actual medicine, but performing magicians in China did start using the mixture in their acts. It would be a few more centuries—around the year 1044— before the Chinese developed the specific formula for gun-powder using those three substances, and that formula is what led to the creation of fireworks. Next time you watch a fireworks display, you can thank a Chinese alchemist!

In the ninth century, an Arabic alchemist and physician named Jābir ibn Hayyān came up with a new theory: Instead of the four or five elements, all metals and minerals were made up of just two, sulfur and mercury. Some metals had more sulfur, while others had more mercury, and Jābir classified—sorted—all of them based on how much of each he thought they contained. Less-pure forms of sulfur and mercury formed more common metals such as iron and lead. Jābir believed that by changing the amount of mercury or sulfur in any kind of metal, he'd be able to turn one type into another. He also thought that creating the purest forms of these metals would produce gold—the alchemist's dream.

All this measuring and classifying of elements sounded like pretty scientific stuff to me, and Dr. Principe agreed. "These alchemists weren't just mixing up what we might call 'witches' brews' of things, hoping that something would come out of it," he said. "They actually had a theory that was based in part on observations. That let them design experiments!"

Unlike the Greeks, who mostly just thought about their alchemy ideas, Jābir actually wanted to test his out in a laboratory. He's credited with saying, "He who makes no experiments will attain nothing." In other words, if you don't test your ideas, you'll never know if they work (which is kind of what Cassie told me about casting spells). Jābir conducted tons of experiments, trying to change the makeup of various metals. He'd heat them up or try to dissolve them or make various combinations to see what would happen, and he kept lots and lots of notes. Jābir's theories on mercury and sulfur lasted for nearly a thousand years, into the 1700s, after which more modern science techniques showed his ideas to be incorrect. Even so, his methodical and well-documented work ended up being extremely useful. For starters, he invented new types of laboratory equipment that would help him run his tests, such as the alembic—two glass bottles connected by a tube that could be used for separating the different types of liquids in a mixture. Even now, chemistry labs use a more modern version of this device.

He also came up with several important methods that today's scientists still use, including:

CRYSTALLIZATION
a method for transforming a liquid into a solid

DISTILLATION
the process of separating out two or more liquids from a mixture

SUBLIMATION
where a solid substance changes into a gas without first becoming a liquid (for example: dry ice)

EVAPORATION
the process of turning a liquid into a gas

IT'S ELEMENTARY!

We already learned that the ancient Greeks believed in four elements—earth, fire, air, and water. They thought that these four items were the essential ingredients that went into creating everything else in the world. It's not a bad idea, and we still use this concept of ingredients to explain nature. However, instead of the four classical elements, modern scientists use chemical elements, and there are a lot more than four of them.

Maybe you've heard of something called the periodic table? This is a chart of the known chemical elements that make up all matter in the universe. Matter is anything around us that takes up space, everything that we can see, feel, taste, touch—and even some of the stuff we can't. All matter is made of atoms, the infinitesimally small particles that are the universe's building blocks. There are ninety-two different kinds of atoms that occur naturally—there are also several kinds made by humans in labs—and each specific type is known as an element. Each chemical element listed on the periodic table is made up of only one kind of atom.

Nickel is an element. So is iron. Steel is not, because it has both nickel and iron in it, which makes it a compound. Aluminum cans, which sound like they're made of only one element—aluminum—are also compounds, because they contain a tiny bit of another element known as magnesium. By combining elements with one another, scientists can create new substances through something called a chemical reaction. But chemical reactions can't turn one kind of element into another.

Why? It has to do with the even smaller ingredients that make up atoms—tiny particles called electrons, protons, and neutrons. These three particles—known as subatomic particles—are found in every type of atom on Earth, and the number of protons and neutrons an atom has defines what kind of element it is. That number can't be changed with chemical reactions, and since lead is an element, and so is gold, turning lead into gold is impossible . . .

. . . unless, as we learned in chapter 1, you have an atom smasher. But that's a story for another time.

PERIODIC TABLE OF THE ELEMENTS

LEGENDS:

Atomic Number — 4
Symbol — Be
Name — Beryllium

1 H Hydrogen
3 Li Lithium
4 Be Beryllium
11 Na Sodium
12 Mg Magnesium
19 K Potassium
20 Ca Calcium
21 Sc Scandium
22 Ti Titanium
23 V Vanadium
24 Cr Chromium
25 Mn Manganese
26 Fe Iron
27 Co Cobalt
28 Ni Nickel
29 Cu Copper
30 Zn Zinc
5 B Boron
6 C Carbon
7 N Nitrogen
8 O Oxygen
9 F Fluorine
2 He Helium
13 Al Aluminum
14 Si Silicon
15 P Phosphorus
16 S Sulfur
17 Cl Chlorine
18 Ar Argon
10 Ne Neon
31 Ga Gallium
32 Ge Germanium
33 As Arsenic
34 Se Selenium
35 Br Bromine
36 Kr Krypton
37 Rb Rubidium
38 Sr Strontium
39 Y Yttrium
40 Zr Zirconium
41 Nb Niobium
42 Mo Molybdenum
43 Tc Technetium
44 Ru Ruthenium
45 Rh Rhodium
46 Pd Palladium
47 Ag Silver
48 Cd Cadmium
49 In Indium
50 Sn Tin
51 Sb Antimony
52 Te Tellurium
53 I Iodine
54 Xe Xenon
55 Cs Caesium
56 Ba Barium
* 57-71
72 Hf Hafnium
73 Ta Tantalum
74 W Tungsten
75 Re Renium
76 Os Osmium
77 Ir Iridium
78 Pt Platinum
79 Au Gold
80 Hg Mercury
81 Tl Thallium
82 Pb Lead
83 Bi Bismuth
84 Po Polonium
85 At Astatine
86 Rn Radon
87 Fr Francium
88 Ra Radium
** 89-103
104 Rf Rutherfordium
105 Db Dubnium
106 Sg Seaborgium
107 Bh Bohrium
108 Hs Hassium
109 Mt Meitnerium
110 Ds Darmstadtium
111 Rg Roentgenium
112 Cn Copernicium
113 Nh Nihonium
114 Fl Flevorium
115 Mc Moscovium
116 Lv Livermoorium
117 Ts Tennessine
118 Og Ognesson

57 La Lanthanum
58 Ce Cerium
59 Pr Praseodymium
60 Nd Neodymium
61 Pm Promethium
62 Sm Samarium
63 Eu Europium
64 Gd Gadolinium
65 Tb Terbium
66 Dy Dysposium
67 Ho Holmium
68 Er Erbium
69 Tm Thallium
70 Yb Ytterbium
71 Lu Luteluim

89 Ac Actinium
90 Th Thorium
91 Pa Protactinium
92 U Uranium
93 Np Neptunium
94 Pu Plutonium
95 Am Americium
96 Cm Curium
97 Bk Berkelium
98 Cf Californium
99 Es Einsteinium
100 Fm Fermium
101 Md Mendelevium
102 No Nobelium
103 Lr Lawrencium

- Non Metals
- Alkaline Earth Metals
- Alkali Metals
- Transition Metals
- Post-Transition Metals
- Metalloids
- Halogens
- Noble Gases
- Actinides
- Lanthanides

Historians credit Jābir with the creation of certain types of acids that became important for chemistry and also for manufacturing. His experiments led to the production of steel and other metals. He figured out how to engrave gold, dye silk and other types of cloth, and make some fabrics waterproof. He discovered how to prevent metals from rusting. And he came up with methods for creating a special type of glass. In today's world, these might not sound all that impressive, but staying dry or preventing tools from rusting would have been a big improvement in the quality of life back then! Jābir's careful way of experimenting, observing, and recording information was definitely scientific, and even though his hypothesis about turning lead into gold wasn't achievable, he still made a lot of important discoveries that we benefit from today.

Now I want to go back to that fifth element that I mentioned earlier—the one that Aristotle thought was the most perfect element ever. He wasn't the only one who believed in its existence. Many different alchemists all over the world believed there was some sort of mysterious material that would help them achieve their goals. In the Middle East, alchemists like Jābir believed in a red powder that came from something called al-iksir. In China, alchemists searched for a substance so pure that adding it to one of their elixirs would result in immortality. And in Europe's Middle Ages—roughly between 500 and 1500—alchemists sought something known as the philosopher's stone, named for the Greek philosophers mentioned earlier in this chapter.

Whoa, whoa, whoa, I thought. ***The philosopher's stone? Isn't that in the Harry Potter books, too?***

Yep! The title of the first Harry Potter book is *Harry Potter and the Sorcerer's Stone* (or *Harry Potter and the Philosopher's Stone*, if you live in England). And sure enough, the philosopher's stone in the book grants whoever uses it eternal life and the ability to turn any kind of metal into gold. It's clear that J. K. Rowling, the author of the Harry Potter books, plucked the idea of the philosopher's stone right out of history.

"The alchemists believed that, supposedly, once you had a little bit of that substance, you could take a big container full of molten lead or boiling mercury and throw just a small crumb of this philosopher's stone into it, and within minutes, it would turn it into gold," Dr. Principe tells me.

In Europe, alchemists tried in vain to either find or create the philosopher's stone. They took the information that alchemists in the Middle East had learned and began to do their own experiments. They came up with rituals and recipes and protected their secrets by writing in code. Part of the reason for all that secrecy was because, at this point in time, it was the Middle Ages, and kings and emperors around Europe had made alchemy illegal. In fact, as we learned in the last chapter, they made *all* magic illegal. In part, this was because they didn't want alchemists to figure out how to make gold and become too wealthy (although kings would often have an official royal alchemist at court, just in case someone finally figured out the answer to this riddle).

But despite alchemy being outlawed, people in Europe (and everywhere else) kept talking about it. They told stories of wizards and sorcerers who possessed the stone and might share bits of it with worthy individuals. There were tales of travelers who journeyed to distant lands and found the philosopher's stone, although—strangely—no one seems to have brought it back with them.

All these stories added to the myths and legends that surrounded alchemy, and it was nearly impossible to tell fact from fiction—science from magic. It also made it hard to know which alchemists were really being scientific about this process (like Jābir) and which were frauds, making fake gold or trying to trick people into paying money in exchange for a fake recipe or a fake philosopher's stone.

"If anything has to do with making gold and money in a short period of time, there are going to be people who try to take advantage of that," Dr. Principe pointed out. "They'd say, 'Oh, I've got the secret—just lend me a little money to help me finish my alchemy research, and then I'll return it and you'll make even more money.' And then you never hear from that 'alchemist' again."

Adding to all this mystery and legend and trickery was one other small problem: Alchemy just didn't seem to work. Although people had been trying for centuries, and there were all kinds of rumors about it being successful, there was no real proof. Alchemy seemed like a total flop, and it's no wonder that people grew a little wary of alchemists.

Eventually, during the Enlightenment period of the 1700s, more modern science techniques finally proved the alchemists' hypotheses wrong. And once people realized that alchemy couldn't work—that it was impossible to chemically change one type of metal into another—they kind of lost interest in it. Alchemy got pushed aside, ignored, and dismissed as "magic"—and kind of silly.

It's true that with the knowledge we have now, turning lead into gold seems like magical thinking, but I can also understand why people might have thought alchemy would work, especially when Dr. Principe told me about an experiment he'd done. While doing some research, he found an old alchemist's recipe from the fourth century, written on a piece of papyrus. It was for something called "divine water." It's made by combining sulfur with quicklime (a chemical found in limestone rocks) and boiling them together in water. Dr. Principe followed the instructions and ended up with this horrible, smelly, orange-red liquid. Then he dipped a silver coin into the liquid to see what would happen.

"It took on a very beautiful gold color," he said. "This was probably once used to make imitation gold. You could take an object, like a medallion, made of silver, dip it in this liquid, and make it look like gold."

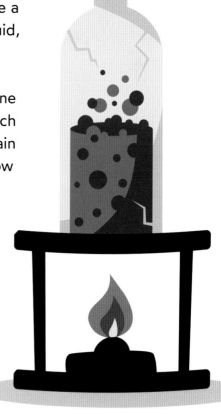

At first glance, it might have seemed like one metal *had* been turned into another—which would have made people all the more certain that alchemy could be done! We now know that this is caused by chemical reactions— and just because something *looks* like gold doesn't mean it is—but that's information people just didn't have back then.

It's amazing that Dr. Principe recreated a recipe over 1,500 years old. And what's even more amazing is that, back then, alchemists didn't have the same tools and instruments that scientists do now, so making divine water—or any other formula—was much harder. They couldn't control temperatures with a thermostat or a dial. That meant they would have had to tend a fire constantly to make sure it stayed at the same temperature.

They also didn't have modern glassware. The kind scientists use in laboratories today doesn't easily crack or chip, and it can be heated over and over again without breaking. But back then, alchemists didn't know how to make that kind of glass yet, so what they used was soft and would shatter easily.

"When I read some of their accounts and notebook entries, their glassware is constantly breaking or exploding or shattering in one way or another, and it must have been incredibly frustrating for them," said Dr. Principe.

You can imagine how exasperated you'd be if every time you tried to finish your math homework, your pencil lead broke! I started to realize that these ancient alchemists were actually really impressive. For thousands of years, alchemists all over the world toiled in laboratories, wrote down their discoveries, and tried to find the philosopher's stone. They were all trying to explain how nature worked and how everything around them fit together to make the world. If we ignore the charlatans (another word for frauds) and tricksters, most alchemists had logical hypotheses that they were trying to test out.

Plus, on top of all that, they helped create a system for doing science that's still important today. The scientific method that we learned about back in chapter 1? Alchemists created that series of steps. They knew they needed to have an organized way of doing experiments, because they wanted to be able to get consistent results that they and others would be able to repeat. And even though they didn't have all the facts or tools we do now, and their understanding of the elements didn't turn out to be correct, they still managed to make many valuable discoveries.

"The alchemists were all about making things," Dr. Principe says. "That could have been gold. It could have been better medicines. It could have been making a cheap purple dye that could compete with the expensive royal purple worn by the emperors. It's taking control over common materials, transforming it in some way into something that is better."

Using mysterious forces to try and control the world around them? That sounds an awful lot like magic—but clearly there's some science in there, too.

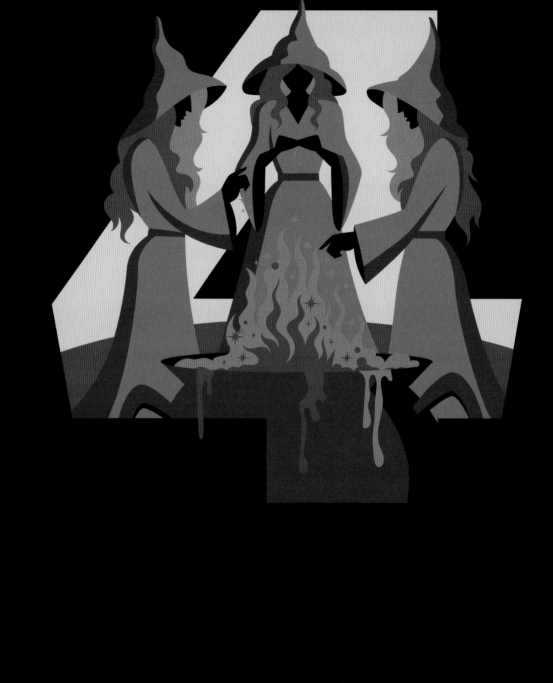

DRINK ME

Double, double toil and trouble;
Fire burn and caldron bubble.
Cool it with a baboon's blood,
Then the charm is firm and good.

Ever heard these lines before? They're from William Shakespeare's play *Macbeth.* It's one of his most famous plays, and since you might not have read it yet, I'll give you an extremely brief summary: After three witches tell him that he will become the ruler of Scotland, a Scottish general named Macbeth and his wife, Lady Macbeth, murder several people to become king and queen. The play itself is much more complex than this, but that's the basic plot. Clearly, Macbeth and his wife are not very nice, but it's still a great story.

There is one scene in the play that has always stuck with me. At the beginning of Act IV, in a dark cave, three witches circle around a bubbling cauldron and mix up a very strange magical potion, while chanting these lines:

Double, double toil and trouble;
Fire burn and caldron bubble.
Fillet of a fenny snake,
In the caldron boil and bake;
Eye of newt and toe of frog,
Wool of bat and tongue of dog,
Adder's fork and blind-worm's sting,
Lizard's leg and howlet's wing,
For a charm of powerful trouble,
Like a hell-broth boil and bubble.

Eye of newt and toe of frog, wool of bat and tongue of dog—*ewwwwww.* That just sounds like the recipe for a really bad stew. It's not clear if Macbeth actually drank this gross concoction (another word for food or drink made of a mix of things), but this scene was exactly what I pictured whenever I thought of magic potions: a big steaming cauldron and some really bizarre ingredients. In fact, it popped into my head when Cassie was reciting her familiar spell, although her mix of ingredients was never meant to be ingested.

Shakespeare probably invented the witches' potion in *Macbeth.* And a lot of the other magic potions I've read about in books or seen in movies also seem entirely made up, especially when you see the recipes for them. There are some pretty horrible-sounding flavors like "bird's tongue" and "frog cheese" and "dragon's teeth." Plus, I'm not even sure where you would get these kinds of things. How do you collect dragon's teeth? Is there a dragon tooth fairy? Do you go to the dragon dentist and ask for the teeth they already pulled? I'd definitely rather let the dentist pull those teeth than do it myself!

Yet, as I started to read more, I learned that at least some of these crazy ingredients could be the names for certain types of plants. Not the official, scientific names, which are usually written in Latin and include a unique combination of two names—kind of like a first and last name—for each species. No, these other names are called folk names, or common names, and a plant can have all kinds of different folk names depending on where it's found and what it looks like.

BINOMIAL NOMENCLATURE

The scientific names of plants—in fact, the scientific names of all living things on Earth—come from a system known as binomial nomenclature. Binomial means "two names," and nomenclature means "the choosing of names." Carolus Linnaeus was a Swedish botanist (a type of scientist that studies plants) who used Latin words to give two names to each of the plants he had studied and collected. Each name includes the genus and species of that particular animal, plant, fungus, or bacteria. You and I are *Homo sapiens*; a domesticated house cat is *Felis catus*.

Since this system is used all over the world, those two names are the same in every country. If a scientist in Finland writes a paper about *Felis catus*, a scientist in China will know exactly what animal that is. This system helps scientists communicate with one another.

LEVELS OF CLASSIFICATION

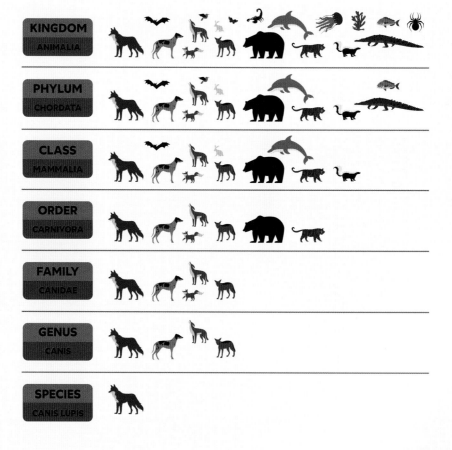

KINGDOM
ANIMALIA

PHYLUM
CHORDATA

CLASS
MAMMALIA

ORDER
CARNIVORA

FAMILY
CANIDAE

GENUS
CANIS

SPECIES
CANIS LUPIS

It also helps them to understand how different living things are related by grouping them together based on shared traits, a process known as biological classification. There are eight main levels of classification: domain, kingdom, phylum, class, order, family, genus, and species. A good way to think about this is to imagine a bookstore. Let's say that our domains—the highest level—are books, magazines, and newspapers, and we're exploring the domain of books. You've got kids' books in one section, adult books in another—you can think of these larger sections like the kingdoms. Then, in each of those kingdoms, there are smaller sections (phylum), like hardcover and paperback. Inside each of those subsections you have fiction and nonfiction (class). And within each of *those*, you have even more categories (order), such as mysteries or poetry. From there, as you get even more specific, you'll narrow it down to types of poetry (family), like rhymed verse. And eventually, you'll end up with just one type (genus), like a limerick. Finally, there is the individual author (species).

Here's a limerick I made up:
A girl found a strange group of creatures,
Didn't know what they were by their features.
Since she thought them unknown,
She took pics with her phone,
And then shared them with her science teachers.

Let's go looking for a plant. I'm going to pick dandelions, since they're all over my yard right now (and the bees love them).

> The most common type of dandelion is in the kingdom *Plantae*, with all the other plants. They're in the phylum *Magnoliophyta*, which is where all flowering plants are found. Their class is *Magnoliopsida*—scientists think this is the most primitive type of flowering plant. Their order is *Asterales*, which includes sunflowers, daisies, and thistles. After order comes family, and dandelions are in the family *Asteraceae*, whose flowers are actually made up of hundreds or even thousands of tiny individual flowers. They're in the genus *Taraxacum*, a group that includes all the different types of dandelions. And the specific species that's in my yard is called *Taraxacum officinale*—the common dandelion.
>
> Those Latin names can be hard to say and remember, so people use the folk names to talk about plants, and, depending on where someone grew up, the folk name they use for a plant might be different from someone else's. Dandelions have been called bitterwort (because they taste bitter), lion's-tooth (because the leaves look like teeth), and puffballs (because of what they look like when they're getting ready to scatter their seeds).

It turns out that dragon's teeth is a type of pea plant with edible seeds. Bird's-tongue isn't actually a bird's tongue; it's a type of plant also known as knotweed, which supposedly helps with tooth problems like plaque. And frog cheese is a fungi—a mushroom—that looks like a big white ball, and some people claim it helps with skin problems.

Oh, that's interesting, I thought. *Some of these magic potion ingredients could actually be a kind of medicine!*

I mean, medicine is basically a mix of ingredients that's supposed to make you feel better. How is a magic potion that's supposed to improve your health any different? We know the ancient Egyptians used a potion of herbs and honey to keep cuts from getting infected. Maybe potions were what we called medicine before we started calling it medicine. Once I started investigating potions, I realized that a lot of them (like the one in Macbeth) were entirely made up. But there were still real ones that humans have used through the centuries, with plants as an essential ingredient.

In fact, plants have always been a big part of our lives, for as long as we've been around. As of today, there are nearly 400,000 species of plants on our planet that we know about, plus lots more we haven't yet discovered and many that have gone extinct over the years. Plants have been around a lot longer than humans. If we look back at Earth's 4.6-billion-year history, land plants—as opposed to plants that grow in water—showed up about 420 million years ago. Our species (*Homo sapiens*) didn't show up until about 300,000 years ago. There's no question that we've always used them for food, fuel, building materials, and health.

I wanted to learn more about plants, medicine, and potions, so I decided to take a trip to the nearby Denver Botanic Gardens. There I met Blake Berger, who'd offered to take me on a tour. Blake is an herbalist—someone who uses plants for healing—and helps to take care of the collection of medicinal plants at the gardens.

"This place is filled with plants that can be used for medicine," Blake told me as we entered the gardens. We walked down a long brick pathway on the first nice day of spring, past flowering trees and new, bright green leaves and tulips of every color imaginable. A cute little bunny (an uninvited guest) munched on some grasses in the warm sun. As we wandered, Blake pointed out several plants that herbalists and botanists would have included in various potions.

"This is comfrey," he told me as he rubbed a leaf between his finger and thumb. "People used to call this bruisewort. They'd take these giant leaves, let them dry, put them in oil, and let them steep for three weeks. Then they'd use that oil—that potion—to heal sprains."

A bit further on, he pointed out a plant called elder, which grows all over the world. "The berries, the flowers, the wood, and the leaves have all been used as medicines," he explained. "Elderberry is especially known for reducing fevers and helping with colds and the flu."

When I looked up both plants online later, I found that scientists had done some experiments to see if they actually worked. With comfrey, scientists proved that an ointment made from the plant's root helped ease painful muscles and joints. And with elder, they found that taking elderberry extract might reduce the length of a cold (although they're still doing more research on this). But what they found pretty clearly demonstrated what herbalists and potion makers already knew.

I wondered how anyone figured this out to begin with. It seems a little risky to walk around munching on random leaves and hoping they'd do more good than harm (and you definitely should not go around sticking unknown plants in your mouth). But how did we learn what plants were safe to eat? What plants might make us sick? And which plants could be useful to our health?

"It took many, many, many generations of trial and error," Blake told me, "to get to the point of where they trusted a plant and knew what it did: if it healed, if it was poisonous, if it wasn't. And I imagine that there were some tragic events that happened along the way."

But we have had thousands and thousands of years to experiment, he pointed out. Back in the Paleolithic—at the same time our ancestors were also making strange things out of ivory—they were undoubtedly using plants.

"Some Neanderthals may have even used herbal medicine," said Blake. "Scientists found cave dwellings where they had been buried with a plant called yarrow, which could help wounds heal."

Of course, this is just an inference—a conclusion reached using evidence and logic.

Scientists don't know for sure that's what the yarrow was for. That kind of information wouldn't have been written down, because writing hadn't been invented yet. Our ancestors would have passed this knowledge down orally, with each generation telling the next what they had learned about the plants around them. Herbalists would have kept careful track of what kinds of plants were useful for food, which ones were poisonous, and which ones could be used to cure illnesses.

"I'd be willing to bet that almost every human knew which plants were useful and what was growing around them," Blake said. "Much more than the modern-day human knows, because back then we were much more reliant upon the land, our surroundings, and what grew."

As we learned back in chapter 2, archaeologists think humans started to use writing about 5,500 years ago, and it looks like we started jotting down our potion recipes not long after that. Around 5,000 years ago, a group of people in Mesopotamia known as the Sumerians wrote about plants on clay tablets and had dozens of formulas using more than 250 plants. The ancient Egyptians wrote about herbal combinations on papyrus and had a list of hundreds of herbal medicines. In India and China, anthropologists have found texts that mention all kinds of herbs. And many of those plants are still used today—like ginger for an upset stomach (think about drinking ginger ale for a stomachache), or parts of the willow tree for aches and pains (the main ingredient in aspirin is extracted from the willow). And those are just two examples of many.

Just recently, I heard about a microbiologist named Dr. Freya Harrison. A microbiologist is a scientist who studies tiny organisms like bacteria and viruses. Dr. Harrison had been looking through medical books

and old crumbling manuscripts from the Middle Ages, trying to find new ideas for killing germs.

Now wait, you might be wondering. ***Don't we have antibiotics and hand sanitizer for that?***

Well, yes, but we have used antibiotics so frequently that many types of bacteria and microbes have become immune to them. These bacteria have mutated—changed—and the antibiotics that used to kill them no longer work. They are what we call drug-resistant or antibiotic-resistant bacteria. Scientists all over the world are trying to find new ways of dealing with this problem of resistance, and some of those new methods might actually be very old ones.

Dr. Harrison came across one book, known as *Bald's Leechbook*, that had been written around the year 950. She wondered if these dusty old pages might hold something useful, like some long-forgotten potion that could be used today. And sure enough, after skipping over the potion that would stop goblins from visiting at night, she found a recipe for something called "Bald's Eyesalve."

The ingredients included onion, garlic, wine, and cow bile—a fluid that is found in the cow's gallbladder (*ew*). Initially I thought it didn't seem like a very hard potion to make—I mean, I can find most of those items in a grocery store (the gallbladder might be tricky). But the ingredients were a little more difficult to find than I'd thought, because Dr. Harrison had to figure out exactly what types of onion and garlic people would have used one thousand years ago. The instructions said to mix them all together and then let the mixture sit in a brass bowl for nine days. The resulting potion could be used to cure an infected eye.

Dr. Harrison realized that each one of those ingredients had anti-bacterial properties; mixed together, they could make for a very potent medicine. When she mixed up a batch and tested it on all kinds of different bacteria—including some that were known to be antibiotic-resistant—it killed the bacteria! Even more interesting was that none of the ingredients were powerful enough on their own. There was something about the combination of *all* of them that made Bald's Eyesalve so effective. This was just an experiment, and scientists are now doing more tests (iterations) to see if this potion can be made into a new antibiotic.

And this isn't the only example of scientists using ancient manuscripts to search for ideas for new medicines. A Chinese researcher named Tu Youyou spent years searching through ancient Chinese texts trying to find a cure for malaria, a deadly disease transmitted through mosquito bites. She found a remedy that required drinking the juice of a plant known as sweet wormwood—and it worked! It became a drug called artemisinin—which is still one of the best defenses we have against malaria—and Tu Youyou won the Nobel Prize in Medicine for her work, despite not being a doctor.

SNAKE OIL

Not all potions are meant to cure people. In fact, they might just be a mishmash of ingredients combined by someone who's only trying to make money and not actually interested in helping people. At best, these potions don't actually do anything, and at worst, they could even make you sick. The people who sell them are often called snake oil salesmen, and those kinds of potions are called snake oil.

But where did that term come from? Back in the mid-1800s, thousands of Chinese people immigrated to the United States to work on building the railroads. They brought their own medicines with them, and among those was actual snake oil. It was made from the oil of a certain kind of Chinese water snake. That oil had anti-inflammatory properties, so it helped with pain and swelling, and it was really, really effective. After long days of extremely dangerous and back-breaking work, the Chinese laborers rubbed the oil on their joints. Historians think that they eventually began to share their snake oil with their American coworkers.

After seeing how helpful it was, *everybody* wanted snake oil. But the Chinese water snake doesn't live in the United States. Some people tried using a different kind of snake to make the oil, but it wasn't nearly as anti-inflammatory. Others saw that so many people wanted snake oil and realized it was a quick way to make money. Take Clark Stanley, for example. He created a product called Stanley's Snake Oil and sold hundreds of bottles in the 1890s. But his potion didn't have a single drop of snake oil in it. It was just made of mineral oil, beef fat, red pepper, and turpentine. People who bought Stanley's oil and other imitation oils didn't get any benefits from using them, because they didn't work.

Eventually the term *snake oil* became associated with fake cures and that reputation stuck (even though actual Chinese snake oil really did work).

The potion masters and herbalists who originally brewed up these concoctions hundreds and hundreds of years ago might not have known *how* the plant remedies worked. They didn't yet have the science to understand the chemical or antibacterial properties of certain plants and potions. But they could definitely see that these mixtures were doing something to make people feel better.

Let's say someone had an upset stomach, and an herbalist gave them a combination of ginger and licorice root. There's evidence that the Chinese used ginger for nausea starting at least two thousand years ago and that people in Ancient Egypt and Ancient India used licorice root for stomach problems. The herbalists in these places didn't know about the specific chemical compounds in ginger and licorice and why those help keep people from throwing up, but they saw that it worked, and they kept using it.

GINGER

"We really didn't know why certain things worked. It was the unexplained, the unknown," said Blake. "It had a much more mysterious aspect to it." He thinks that's part of the reason that the word *potions* makes us think of magic.

LICORICE ROOT

In the case of ginger and licorice root, modern scientists have done tests that prove why these two plants work—mystery solved. But some plants worked for no particular reason, at least not for any reason that can be proved through the scientific method. For example, another remedy in *Bald's Leechbook* said that a person could treat heart pain by boiling a plant called rue in oil and rubbing it on the skin. Scientifically, there's no ingredient in this concoction that should

have helped with heart pain. But mysteriously, this potion could have made people feel better anyway.

Wait, I thought. ***They just felt better for no reason? That definitely sounds like magic.***

Turns out, there's something called the placebo (pluh-SEE-boh) effect: potions and medicines and treatments that shouldn't do anything but still somehow make people feel better. Scientists and doctors have known about the placebo effect for centuries, and probably longer. As far back as the 1700s, there are records of doctors who would prescribe fake medicines—sometimes called placebos or sugar pills— to sick patients when the doctors didn't know of any real medicine that would work. And guess what? They noticed that those patients still improved. They called this the placebo effect—*placebo* means "I please" in Latin.

"It almost seems impossible, like it's magical and mystical," said Dr. Matthew Burke. Dr. Burke is a neurologist—a scientist who studies the brain and the nervous system—who spends a lot of time think-ing about the placebo effect. "But we think there are real scientific reasons behind it that have to do with your brain and how it evolved."

We'll hear more from Dr. Burke in the next chapter, but he told me that scientists don't entirely understand all the details of the placebo effect. They do, however, have some ideas. One is that the medicine works because a patient *believes* it will. They expect that the pill or the plant or the potion will make them feel better, and so their body just starts to feel better on its own, even if they're not getting a real medication. Another possible explanation is that simply seeing a doctor or healer and asking for help will make the patient start to feel better.

Scientists today know that the placebo effect exists and that it's effective. Even if they haven't puzzled out all the reasons why, they don't see it as magic. But I understand why healers and herbalists might have thought it was.

After talking to Blake, it was clear to me that real potions did (and do) exist and that people have used them throughout our history. Plants—and combinations of plants—can help us to get better, which, even if it's scientific, still seems pretty magical. And sometimes, just *thinking* we're going to get better can also help us to improve. Which made me won-der: If our thoughts have that kind of power, what could our words do?

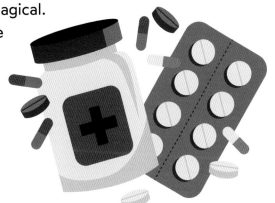

CURSES!

"Words are our most powerful magic," Cassie had told me as we sat on the floor of her living room. It was a saying inspired by *Harry Potter and the Deathly Hallows*, but the idea that words have power is something she'd always felt was important whenever she cast a spell. "A lot of magic and witchcraft is about paying attention to the words you use in a spell and being careful about the words you choose."

So far, the words that Cassie had uttered during our spell-casting ceremony hadn't worked yet. It had been a couple of weeks, and I still hadn't seen signs of a familiar—just a *lot* of moths invading my house as they made their annual migration. But I was intrigued by the idea of the power of words. I thought about how when someone gives me a compliment or says I did a great job on something, it makes me feel pretty good. And then I thought about the opposite of that. When someone says something mean, that can make me feel pretty awful. So words clearly have an effect on people—what about curses? Do those really exist? The way I understood it, a curse is a type of spell that uses words or phrases to cause someone else to have bad luck, like an injury or an illness. I looked around online and found out that the word *curse* comes from the Old English word *curs,* which meant to wish evil or harm on someone.

Of course, there are lots of examples of this in movies and books— think of poor Sleeping Beauty who pricked her finger on a spinning wheel and fell into a deep sleep because of a curse. And, since Cassie mentioned Harry Potter, in those books there are all kinds of curses, like the Cruciatus Curse (which inflicts terrible pain), the Imperius Curse (which causes the victim to be completely obedient), and the Killing Curse (which causes instant death).

Using words to make people do what you want—or even die? I thought that seemed unlikely, but I was still curious. We've all probably had a moment or two where we've wished someone ill or had a not-so-nice outburst or thought. Those are pretty informal curses. Some curses are much more elaborate, like the curse tablets in Ancient Rome that we learned about earlier. And the anthropologists and archaeologists I talked to said that using curses—whether you just muttered them under your breath, or took part in some sort of ritual—was a pretty common practice that people all over the world took part in.

CURSED OBJECTS

It's not just people and places that can be cursed—so can objects. Here are a few supposedly cursed objects and the stories behind them.

THE HOPE DIAMOND—This large blue diamond was supposedly found in India in the mid-1600s.

THE CURSE: Over the centuries, it has had many owners—but at a price. According to the legend, anyone who owns or wears this precious gem will be doomed to tragedy. Newspaper stories from the early 1900s give a long list of owners who were killed or thrown in prison, or who had lost their fortunes.

THE TRUTH: Most of the stories turned out to be made up, either by the owners (who wanted the gem to seem more mysterious) or by newspapers (who wanted people to buy copies of the paper). In 1958, the diamond's last owner, a jeweler named Harry Winston, donated it to the Smithsonian's National Museum of Natural History in Washington, DC, and you can go see it to this day.

THE GREAT BED OF WARE—A huge, wooden four-poster bed (a type of bed with four columns, one in each corner) built in England around 1590. It's so big that supposedly eight people can sleep in it at once!

THE CURSE: Jonas Fosbrooke, the carpenter who made the bed, intended it for King Edward IV. However, the bed ended up at an inn, where the commoners who were allowed to sleep in it covered it with carvings and graffiti. Fosbrooke's angry ghost supposedly attacked anyone not of royal blood who slept in the bed.

THE TRUTH: The bed was probably built as a tourist attraction for the local inn (and it did become quite famous—even Shakespeare wrote about it). But even if Fosbrooke's ghost is upset, no one is sleeping in the bed anymore now that it's in the Victoria and Albert Museum in London.

***THE CRYING BOY* PAINTING**—A painting made in the 1950s by an Italian painter named Giovanni Bragolin. The painting was extremely popular, and many people had copies of it in their homes.

THE CURSE: In England, firefighters found undamaged copies of *The Crying Boy* in several houses that had burned down. Rumors circulated that the painting—supposedly cursed by the boy depicted in it—would burn down any house it hung in.

> THE TRUTH: The painting was so popular that it hung in thousands and thousands of homes, so it's not surprising that it was found in homes that burned down. In addition, a local fire chief said the paintings had been printed on a type of material that didn't burn easily, which is why they tended to survive the fires.

In fact, Dr. Gosden (the archaeologist who wrote about the history of magic) told me that pretty much wherever archaeologists have found records of writing, they've found evidence of curses, too. Some of the oldest curse stories come from Egypt. Tori Finlayson is studying to become an Egyptologist—a scientist who is an expert on Ancient Egypt—and she has been on several expeditions to Egypt where she explored temples that are thousands of years old. She told me about special objects, called execration figurines, that people would use to curse others or that the government would use to curse enemies of the state.

"They're basically an image or a small doll that represents your enemy, and you do horrible things to them," she told me. "You curse them verbally, spit on them or step on them, and then you bury them in the ground or in a cemetery wall. And that keeps the curse going for eternity."

Tori also told me that Egyptians would curse people who had already died by erasing their name from their tomb and from everywhere it had been written down. Egyptians believed that someone who had died would go to the underworld—this was very important to them—and that if you erased all records of a person's existence on

Earth, they wouldn't exist in the afterlife, either. Additionally, if there was no evidence a person had ever been alive, that person would eventually be forgotten—which also seems like a form of punishment, because most people want to be remembered.

"Names and language are really important to the Egyptians," said Tori. "Even today, language is still pretty powerful." Saying someone's name or cursing them was a way of trying to have control over them, she pointed out. This reminded me of what Dr. Gosden had said earlier about why people used magic: because they wanted to feel like they had a little bit of control.

Back in Ancient Egypt, people were more likely to speak their curses out loud than they were to write them down, Tori told me. Most people then couldn't read or write. But there are still plenty of written curses, and archaeologists have found some of the oldest known curses inscribed on the walls and doorways of the tombs of ancient Egyptians. One tomb—from somewhere between 2686 and 2160 BCE, more than four thousand years ago—belonged to a man who had helped build the pyramids in Giza. His name was Petety, and he'd been buried with his wife. Outside the entrance to their tombs, Egyptologists found several curses carved in the stone, meant to discourage people from disturbing their graves. One of these curses read:

> *Oh, all the people who enter this tomb,*
> *Who will make evil against this tomb, and destroy it:*
> *May the crocodile be against them on water,*
> *And snakes against them on land.*
> *May the hippopotamus be against them on water,*
> *The scorpion against them on land.*

This curse sounded like the exact opposite of Cassie's familiar spell! Thankfully, the scientists who found the tomb didn't report any attacks by crocodiles or hippopotamuses, so it doesn't seem like the curse worked, or at least it didn't last for four thousand years. But it may have lasted long enough to keep grave robbers out of the tomb—allowing archaeologists to find and study Petety and his wife's remains.

I also heard about another curse Egyptologists had supposedly found in a tomb belonging to King Tutankhamen (King Tut for short). He lived around 1300 BCE and became the king of Egypt when he was only nine years old. Unfortunately, he didn't reign for terribly long—only about ten years. He died at the age of nineteen, probably of malaria or some sort of other infection. He received a royal burial in the appropriately named Valley of the Kings, in the deserts of southern Egypt. His followers filled his tomb with chariots, furniture, golden statues, daggers, board games, clothing, shoes, and ornate jewelry.

This wasn't all that unusual—most royalty received lavish burials like this, and these were the things the Egyptians thought kings and queens might want in the afterlife. But you know who else might want them? Grave robbers. All those items were pretty valuable—especially the gold—so robbers would often raid the tombs after they'd been sealed up and make off with all the loot.

But unlike the other royal tombs in the Valley of the Kings, grave robbers never found King Tut's. No one did—until 1922, when a British Egyptologist by the name of Howard Carter discovered the entrance to the tomb with the help of a local twelve-year-old

Egyptian boy named Hussein Hassan Abdel Rassuhl. It's at this moment that the story of the curse begins. Within a few months of the discovery, Lord Carnarvon—Howard Carter's boss and the man who had paid for the search for Tut's tomb—died from an infected mosquito bite. Carnarvon's half-brother died a few months after that. Another Egyptologist who had been helping Carter died a week before they finished examining all the objects in the tomb. And over the years, several of the American and British visitors to the tomb also became ill and died. People began to think that the ancient Egyptians had placed some sort of curse on Tut's grave—a curse that affected those who disturbed the boy king's final resting place.

The idea intrigued a lot of people, many of whom believed the story to be true. Newspapers published articles about the "curse of the pharaohs," and even to this day, people talk about the curse of King Tut's tomb.

But unlike at Petety's tomb, no one ever found a curse inscribed anywhere in King Tut's tomb. And there were a lot of people who worked on King Tut's tomb, as well as lots of other tombs and temples, who never got sick. In fact, nothing happened to the majority of those people—including all the people who had helped unwrap King Tut's mummy.

THE THREE Cs

So how do we explain all the people who died or got hurt after the opening of King Tut's tomb? It helps to think about the three Cs—causation, correlation, and coincidence.

CAUSATION is when one event causes another event. An easy example is if it's raining outside, you'll get wet. In this case, it's a very clear causation—if you go outside while it's pouring cats and dogs, you will definitely get soaked.

CORRELATION means there's a relationship between two events, but one doesn't necessarily cause the other. For instance, let's say you read an article that says that when people eat ice cream, they're more likely to get stung by a bee. This doesn't mean that ice cream itself causes the bee stings. Think about it: People are more likely to eat ice cream cones in the summer, and they're more likely to be outside in the summer. Guess what else is outside in the summer? Bees. Ice cream and bee stings are correlated—they happen at the same time and are both related to summer—but one doesn't actually cause the other.

COINCIDENCE is when two events happen at the same time and are not related at all. Maybe you were thinking of your favorite song and then, a few minutes later, it came on the radio. It's pretty unlikely that the radio station heard your brain waves, so the fact that your favorite song started to play is just coincidence.

Now let's take King Tut's tomb: Archaeologists opened King Tut's tomb. Some people died afterward. According to the idea of the curse, opening King Tut's tomb caused those people to die. But if you look at just the facts, there is no clear causation. In fact, scientists and archaeologists who looked into the curse found no relationship between the two, and ten years after the tomb was opened, almost all the people who had been there were still alive. That means the relationship between the opening of King Tut's tomb and the deaths of several people aren't at all related and can be chalked up not to a curse, but a coincidence.

Many people were convinced the curse of the pharaohs was real. This is partly because it's a good story—a little bit creepy, a little bit scary, and definitely mysterious. Just the kind of story that people like to read about (but don't like to actually have happen to them). But the other reason people may have thought the story was true is because there have been real-life examples of curses that seemingly caused people to die or become very sick.

One of the most interesting ones I read about happened back in 1938 in Selma, Alabama. Dr. Drayton Doherty had a patient by the name of Vance Vanders at one of the hospitals in town. The man had been sick for weeks and lost about fifty pounds, but no one could figure out why. All the tests and X-rays came back normal. He didn't appear to have any of the diseases that might cause something like this to happen to him, but he wouldn't eat, and every time he did, he threw up.

It seemed likely that Mr. Vanders was going to die, and Dr. Doherty didn't know what to do. Then Mrs. Vanders—Vance's wife—quietly told Dr. Doherty that, about four months earlier, her husband had gotten into an argument with the local Vodou priest. Vodou is a type of religion that began centuries ago in West Africa and was later brought to the Americas by African people who had been forced into slavery. The word *vodou* means "spirit" in a West African language known as Fon. Vodou is still practiced in West Africa, as well as in South America, Central America, and North America, where the descendants of those original enslaved Africans live.

In communities that practice Vodou, there are priests and priestesses that lead religious rituals, heal sick people—and sometimes curse them. The Vodou priest that Mr. Vanders argued with did just that, and told him he wouldn't live long. Dr. Doherty listened carefully to the story and realized that Mr. Vanders truly believed in the curse, which is what had made him so ill. But what could the doctor do?

The next morning, Dr. Doherty told the entire family to come to the hospital. He told them a story about how he had gone to the graveyard the night before to confront the Vodou priest about his curse on Mr. Vanders. At first, the priest refused to share the details of what he'd done, but Dr. Doherty said he'd forced the priest to tell him everything.

"That Vodou priest rubbed some lizard eggs into your skin," Dr. Doherty explained to the family. "They climbed down into your real stomach and hatched out some small lizards. All but one of them died, leaving one large one, that is eating up all your food and the lining of your body. I will now get that lizard out of your system and cure you of this horrible curse."

Dr. Doherty asked a nurse to come into the room. He'd arranged with her beforehand to fill a syringe with an emetic—a medicine that causes people to vomit. He took the syringe and injected it into Mr. Vanders's arm. Minutes later, Mr. Vanders began to throw up. A lot. And when it looked like he was just about done, Dr. Doherty secretly pulled a small green lizard out of his bag and dropped it into the basin, while exclaiming, "Look, Vance, look what has come out of you. You are now cured. The Vodou curse is lifted!"

Mr. Vanders fell back on the bed and went into a deep sleep. When he awoke the next morning, he ate for the first time in weeks. A week later, he left the hospital and eventually gained back all the weight he'd lost. Even though Dr. Doherty never actually confronted the Vodou priest—he had made up the whole story and snuck in the lizard—he made Mr. Vanders *believe* the curse had been broken.

WHAT'S THE MAGIC WORD?

Abracadabra! A la peanut butter sandwiches! Open sesame!

The idea of pointing a magic wand at something and shouting or whispering strange words is familiar. We see wizards do it in movies, and magicians do it on stage. We might even say those words ourselves as we wave our hands and wait for the automatic doors to slide open at the grocery store. (I've done this—have you?)

But magic words aren't just found in stories or movies or magic shows. People all over the world use magic words, for a variety of purposes. Some are meant to protect people and their belongings from fire, curses, or theft. Others are supposed to bring good luck. A handful supposedly call on supernatural beings for help. They can be found in a variety of languages, although the spellings may have changed as people passed the words down through generations or shared them with different cultures. Some are written in code. Some are complete gibberish—nonsense words and syllables (or at least that's what they seem like to us now).

One of the most famous magic words is *abracadabra*. It's been around since the second century BCE and was known as a magical word for healing, but no one knows for sure where it came from originally. The word appears written as an inverted pyramid, getting shorter and shorter with each line:

As the word shrinks, your aches, pains, and fever were supposed to decrease as well.

There are thousands of magic words, and many of us use magic words every day—including you. After all, *please* and *thank you* are among the most powerful words in the English language.

This story is **bananas**, I thought. *How could just words almost scare someone to death?*

To find out how this works, I talked once more to Dr. Matthew Burke, the neuroscientist we heard from briefly in the last chapter. He told

me that when people genuinely believe they've been cursed, they can actually get quite sick. It's called the nocebo (no-SEE-boh) effect, *nocebo* meaning "I will be harmful" in Latin. We already learned about the placebo effect—when people start to feel better even if the medication or treatment they've been given is fake. The nocebo effect is the opposite—it's sometimes called the placebo effect's evil twin!

There are other examples of the nocebo effect happening with curses, like the one that affected Mr. Vanders. But Dr. Burke told me that scientists most often see the nocebo effect when new medications are tested to see if they work. During these tests, some people will be given the real medication, and some people will be given a sugar pill. This is a fake medication that shouldn't have any effect on the body. None of the people participating in the tests know if they've gotten the real medicine or the fake one.

As part of the tests, the doctors have to tell everyone who is involved about any possible side effects of the real medication—even if they're just getting the sugar pill. And in the case of the nocebo effect, a patient who gets the sugar pill might still report having side effects— nausea, dizziness, a rash. They believe they're taking the real medication, and so they believe they are experiencing the real side effects. Something is happening in the brain that actually causes the person to have physical problems, even if there's no reason for it.

"Let's look at the case of Mr. Vanders," said Dr. Burke. "He genuinely believed he'd been cursed. Even if it sounds wacky or supernatural to us, he believed it, and it was enough to change his brain." Luckily, Dr. Doherty understood that the curse felt real to Mr. Vanders and knew that the best way to help him would be to do something to make him believe the curse had been lifted.

If I hadn't believed in curses before, I definitely did after hearing the story of Mr. Vanders. Cassie was right: Words can have a really strong effect on people, which is a good reason to be careful about what you say. I thought back to what Dr. Gosden said about how if you *believe* in magic, you think things like curses or killing a chicken a certain way might have an effect. I'd been defining magic as the idea that humans can use mysterious forces to control the world around them. Those forces may not always line up with how we think about science, but even so, it sounds like that doesn't mean they don't work, especially if we believe.

So curses do work sometimes. Potions do, too. I could see why the placebo and nocebo effects might seem like magic to people—they certainly felt that way to me. And because they're based on personal feelings, rather than facts, I could also see why scientists might have trouble using the scientific method to study them. A scientist might ask the question, "Will this curse make a person sick?" And let's say that the curse seems to work on one person, who does become ill. A responsible scientist would then repeat the experiment multiple times, with different people, to see if they get the same result. If I believe someone has the power to curse me and make me sick, I'm more likely to become sick. If I don't believe that, then the curse probably won't work. A curse is based on personal feelings, rather than facts—it's subjective—so getting the same result over and over will be harder.

Still, as Dr. Burke pointed out, there are good scientific reasons for why curses are effective (just like with the placebo effect and potions), even though scientists don't entirely understand what's happening in the brain. It seems that a lot of what I'd considered magic happens in the brain—it's about what a person feels or believes—and this definitely seemed to be the case with superstitions.

KNOCK ON WOOD

Have you ever avoided walking under a ladder? Or jumped over a crack so you didn't step on it? Do you have a lucky piece of clothing that you wear when you have a test or a big game? Do you say "Bless you!" when someone sneezes? Or do you think that if a ladybug lands on you, it'll bring good luck? If so, you're at least a little superstitious! A superstition is a belief in something that doesn't follow the rules of science and is generally considered irrational, or not logical. Despite this, superstitions are everywhere, and you've probably come across them more often than you realize.

If you remember back to your last birthday, you might have had candles on your cake. You may have heard the superstition that your wish won't come true if you don't blow them all out in one breath. Sadly, it has become harder for me to do this because I now have too many candles on my cake (which is probably why I didn't get the pony I asked for).

Now do I actually think that if I blew out those candles all at once, my wish would come true? Well, no. Not really. But there is a tiny part of me that always hopes it will. It's the same part that thinks seven is a lucky number, has me make a wish when the clock reads 11:11, and picks up pennies for luck.

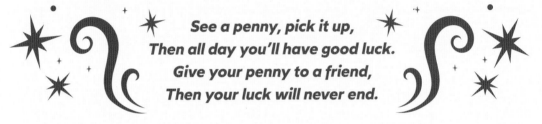

See a penny, pick it up,
Then all day you'll have good luck.
Give your penny to a friend,
Then your luck will never end.

I don't actually think my day-to-day existence is going to change by doing these things, but I figure it can't hurt, right? Picking up the penny probably isn't going to make things worse, and there's the tiny (magical) chance that things might get better.

On the flip side, I definitely avoid walking under ladders, because I've always heard it's bad luck. But why would that one small action bring bad luck? Who came up with that idea? I'm sure that it's partially because there's always the chance someone will drop something on you. Or you might bump the ladder and accidentally hurt the person on it. So in a way, the ladder superstition is just smart thinking. The same goes for the superstition about opening an umbrella in the house. You're way more likely to poke someone or knock something over by unfurling your bumbershoot indoors. Yes, both of those actions could bring bad luck by causing an accident, but they could also be avoided—just take that umbrella outside!

Some of these superstitions might just be about good sense and don't have much to do with bad luck. I wasn't sure I'd even call them superstitions. But there were a few that seemed to be more irrational. Take, for instance, the belief that breaking a mirror brings seven years of bad luck. Where did that come from? Obviously, you don't want to break one, because there'll be shards of glass everywhere, but how does luck factor in? One possibility is that the ancient Romans, who were the first people to create mirrors using metal, thought that damaging one was disrespectful and would anger the gods.

Humans all over the world are also superstitious about numbers. In Western countries, the number thirteen is considered unlucky. You may have noticed that there isn't a button for the thirteenth floor in the elevator of some tall buildings, and often, there isn't a row thirteen on an airplane. In China, four is unlucky (because it's pronounced the same way as the word for death), while the number eight is a very lucky number—people try to get phone numbers with as many eights in them as possible, and officials specifically scheduled the Beijing Summer Olympics to start on August 8, 2008 (8-8-08)!

I also read a superstition about sneezing that says that when you *achoo!*, all the air in your body is expelled, and you might end up sucking in a demon when you inhale again. That's why we say "Bless you!" when someone sneezes— to keep the evil spirits from invading their body (although most people probably don't even know about that part of it). There are others, too, finding a four-leaf clover, tossing a pinch of salt over your shoulder if you spill some, placing a "beckoning cat" in your home or business to invite luck in, hanging horseshoes above a door with the ends up (to keep the luck in)—the list goes on and on. But when we stop to think about it logically—*Are demons really going to invade someone's body right after they sneeze? Is luck actually going to fall out of a horseshoe?*—these kinds of superstitions do sound a bit silly.

So if superstitions aren't rational, and they don't actually cause things to happen, good or bad, then why do we still believe in them? To answer this question, I talked to Dr. Stuart Vyse. He's a psychologist—a scientist who studies the way people think, feel, and behave—and he's written several books about superstition and magic and why we believe in both.

"Many things happen in life," he explained. "They can be bad things, like illness and accidents. Or they can be good things. Making sure that you avoid the bad and achieve the good is why, when they don't really have any control, people will start to use superstitions."

That sounded an awful lot like some of the reasons I'd heard earlier for why humans have practiced magic throughout history. Trying to bring in good luck (while avoiding bad luck) has a lot to do with wanting to have some control of what's happening around you. And,

Dr. Vyse told me, superstitions might be one of the earliest forms of magical thinking, since they're part of how we evolved. Because humans don't have fur or claws or fangs or shells, we don't have a lot of protection from the world. Instead, we have to rely on our brains to learn how to survive, and because of that, we're always gathering lots of information about what's going on around us. We're looking for patterns—if we can recognize them, we can know when things are "normal" and "not normal" and be better prepared.

Here's a common example of this: If you live in an area that has mountain lions roaming around (or you've watched a lot of nature documentaries about mountain lions), your brain might automatically assume that rustling grass is a sign that one is nearby. Let's say you're out for a walk in the tall grass and there's a rustle nearby. You could assume that it's nothing—that it's just the wind. Or you could assume that there's a mountain lion in that grass. If you assume it's just the wind, you might be right . . . or you might be wrong. If you always think a rustle in the grass is a predator, you're going to run away, and you're more likely to survive. Even if it's not a mountain lion, your brain wants you to act as though there is one and run away, so you can live another day. After all, it's better to be safe than sorry.

What does this have to do with superstitions? Dr. Vyse told me that sometimes humans see these kinds of patterns where there aren't any. That means we sometimes think two unrelated things *are* related. With negative superstitions, people notice that something bad happened and want to find a reason for why things went wrong, probably because they hope to avoid that bad thing happening again in the future. For instance, maybe you dropped your ice cream cone one day. And just before that happened, you stepped on a crack. You might wonder if the two are related—is it causation, correlation, or coincidence? You don't know for sure, so maybe in the future you'll take extra care to avoid cracks when you're eating ice cream. It's better to think that you can avoid bad luck by taking some sort of action than it is to think that sometimes bad things just happen.

With positive superstitions, something good has happened to you, and again, you're trying to figure out what caused it. If you can find a pattern, then you might be able to make that good thing happen regularly, even if what you did really had nothing to do with why something good happened. For instance, let's say you have a lucky rabbit's foot (which, if you think about it, was very *unlucky* for the rabbit). And let's say that one day you decide to bring your lucky rabbit's foot with you to school because you have a big math test. *It can't hurt. Maybe it will help?* you wonder. And guess what? You do really well on the math test. You get an A! Then the next time you have a math test, you bring your lucky rabbit's foot with you to school again, and you get another A.

If this worked for my math test, then maybe it will work for my English test, too, you think. Sure enough, you get an A on the English test! You start carrying your lucky rabbit's foot to school for *all* your tests.

Then one day—the day of your history test—you forget your lucky rabbit's foot. Uh-oh. Your test comes back, and you didn't do as well—you got a C+. *If only I'd brought my lucky rabbit's foot, I would have aced it!* you think. The next history test, you double-check to make sure that Thumper (as you've taken to calling your lucky rabbit's foot) is in your bag. The test comes back with an A.

So now your brain thinks there's a pattern: Bring the lucky rabbit's foot and get an A; forget it and get a C. You've created a superstition for yourself. What's interesting is that you see a connection between the lucky rabbit's foot and your grades, but you're kind of ignoring the fact that you also studied really hard for all these exams, so your grades might have more to do with your actual studying than they do with Thumper. However, now that you've associated Thumper with your good test scores, you're going to have a hard time getting rid of this superstition.

SPORTS SUPERSTITIONS

Athletes (and their fans) might be some of the most superstitious people out there. Many of them perform certain rituals before every game, hoping to boost their chances at winning (although they also practice really hard). Here are a few of them:

- Former Chicago Bulls basketball player Michael Jordan always wore his college basketball shorts underneath his Chicago Bulls shorts during games.

- Serena Williams, a professional tennis player and one of the greatest athletes of all time, wore the same pair of socks for every match of a tournament and didn't wash them until she lost.

- No one knows for sure how this superstition got started, but it's apparently very unlucky to bring peanuts that are still in their shells to an auto race (peanut M&Ms are OK, though).

- Wade Boggs, who played for the Boston Red Sox, wore the same socks for every game, fielded exactly 150 ground balls at every practice, and always ate a lot of chicken before every game (he later wrote a chicken cookbook).

- Czech Olympic snowboarder Eva Samková Adamczyková draws a fake mustache on her upper lip before she competes in big events—and she wore it to accept a gold medal in the 2014 Winter Olympics.

I understand why people want to find patterns and connections. It's part of how we learn, and it's been important to our survival. And yes, sometimes we find patterns and connections where there aren't any. But some of these connections seemed kind of far-fetched, like associating good test scores with carrying Thumper rather than all the studying. Why would we pick superstition over what makes the most sense?

One reason, Dr. Vyse told me, might have to do with what's going on in the world around us. He said that in countries that are experiencing war or having economic problems, more people say they believe in superstitions—probably because they don't feel like they have any control over these kinds of really big problems. Superstitions and magical beliefs tend to be more popular when people feel stressed or when they feel uncertain about the outcome of something. That's why some of the most superstitious people are students (who worry about how they'll perform on a test) and athletes (who aren't sure how they'll do during an important game).

But what I found really interesting is that, in some cases, those superstitions can actually be helpful! A group of scientists in Germany wanted to know more about superstitions, so they designed an experiment to test what effect lucky objects have on people. In one study, they asked the participants to bring a personal lucky charm with them to take a couple of tests. For each test, some of the people were allowed to keep their lucky charm, while others had theirs taken away. One was a memory test, in which the participants had to match pairs of shapes (much like the card game Memory, if you've ever played that). The other one involved creating as many words as possible out of a list of eight letters. Both of these tests were timed.

And guess what? Those who had been allowed to keep their lucky charms did better than the ones who didn't. The scientists who planned the study now have a theory that superstitious beliefs might actually make a person believe more in their own talents and abilities. While Thumper probably has nothing to do with how well-prepared you are for your test—and you don't actually need it because you studied, right?—if you have it with you on the day of the big test, you might feel more confident about getting the answers right, and you might actually do better.

"Superstitions come from a lack of control over what's happening in the world," he explained.

Whether you're avoiding cracks or bringing Thumper to school, you're *doing* something, you're taking action—and that gives you an illusion of control. As he pointed out earlier, that's one of the reasons we have superstitions—we want to feel like we have some control—and that seems to be a big part of magic in general.

"But hopefully students don't give up on studying and just bring a rabbit's foot to their test instead," said Dr. Vyse, laughing. "It's fun to pretend that these small actions might change the outcomes of events, but it's important to remember that they don't actually make that much of a difference. They're not actually magic."

I know that, in reality, when I knock on wood or throw spilled salt over my shoulder, those actions aren't changing anything. But I also know that I will probably keep doing them. Yes, superstitions might be a little silly, but there's still a tiny part of me that thinks, *Can't hurt. Might help.* I'll keep crossing my fingers. Just in case.

I KNOW WHAT YOU'RE THINKING

"OK, Laura—take this book and flip through it, because I want you to be able to verify that it's not the same page over and over again."

On a rainy April evening, I sat in a darkened theater with a small group of about fifteen other people. We were at a magic show, and in front of us, dressed head to toe in all black, stood Joe Diamond. He had friendly, mischievous eyes and a cheerful face. To his right was a round table filled with a variety of objects—decks of cards, a small manila envelope, books, wooden boxes, a small chalkboard, and what looked like a weird wine glass.

That might seem like an odd assortment of items, but Joe is a magician, and he'd just handed me one of the books from his prop table. It was a collection of Sherlock Holmes mystery stories by Sir Arthur Conan Doyle (who was fascinated by magic). Joe asked me to flip through the pages to make sure it was a real book and not a trick prop. It looked real to me, with regular words and sentences. I even recognized some of the story titles.

"Now open it up to any page you want, and pick a word. I won't look, so I won't know if you're at the beginning, middle, or end of the book. Let me know when you find a nice, big, long, interesting word—but don't tell me what that word is."

He turned dramatically and looked in the complete opposite direction as I did what I was told. I chose a page near the beginning of the book and focused on a word about halfway down. Then I shut the book. There were so many words in this collection of stories, and so

many pages, that there was no way he would be able to guess which one I'd picked.

Joe stared at me thoughtfully and then said, "Your word starts with an M or a P, is that correct?"

I was flabbergasted. He was right—it started with an M.

He paused and gazed off into space for a minute, with his finger on his chin.

"If I'm correct, just hand the book back to me. I believe you are thinking of the word *mourning*."

My jaw dropped open. I handed the book back to Joe.

Whoa! I thought. ***Did he really just read my mind? How did he do that?***

That trick took place about halfway through Joe's show, and it only got more amazing from there. He had one audience member pick a card, and then somehow knew what card it was. He correctly guessed the numbers that people wrote down on small pieces of paper and put in their pockets. He zapped away people's strength with a special metal wand!

You can imagine that, by the time the show ended, I was incredibly curious about how Joe had pulled off all those tricks. And were they *actually* tricks? They seemed so believable! Magicians, of course, don't like to reveal their secrets. They want their audience to believe that what's happening on stage might be real. Or, even if people don't think it's real, magicians want them to at least be amazed and to wonder how the trick was done. That's part of the fun of being a magician—knowing something that no one else does and getting the audience to believe what they're seeing.

THE MAGICIAN'S OATH

Do you want to be a magician? Then you're going to have to take an oath!

As a magician, I promise never to reveal the secret of any illusion to a non-magician, unless that one swears to uphold the Oath in turn. I promise never to perform any illusion for any non-magician without first practicing the effect until I can perform it well enough to maintain the illusion of magic.

These two sentences are known as the Magician's Oath. The language has changed over time, but the idea behind it remains the same: Anyone learning to do a magic trick has to promise that they won't share the secrets of how to do that trick with anyone else. In the past, before there were books and websites about how to do magic tricks, magicians would have handed tricks down from one generation to the next, and they would have wanted to ensure that the tricks were done properly and that their students didn't give away their secrets.

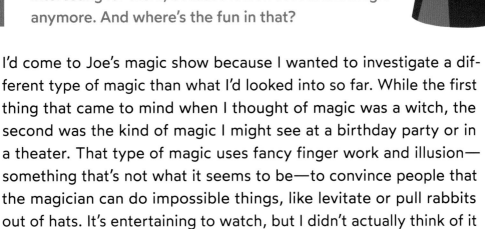

This, of course, makes a lot of sense. If performing magic is your job, you don't want everyone to know exactly how you do what you do. You also don't want other magicians going out there and performing the tricks that you spent so much time mastering. Also, if the audience knows all the tricks and how the magician does them, it's not going to be very interesting for them, because it won't seem like magic anymore. And where's the fun in that?

I'd come to Joe's magic show because I wanted to investigate a different type of magic than what I'd looked into so far. While the first thing that came to mind when I thought of magic was a witch, the second was the kind of magic I might see at a birthday party or in a theater. That type of magic uses fancy finger work and illusion—something that's not what it seems to be—to convince people that the magician can do impossible things, like levitate or pull rabbits out of hats. It's entertaining to watch, but I didn't actually think of it as being anything more than a performance.

But while I watched the show, I kept thinking back to my definition of magic—something that seems to use mysterious forces to control the world and that doesn't match up with how we think science works. Knowing what word people secretly picked out of a book or using a wand to weaken them sure seems to match that definition. Based on what I knew about science, I was pretty sure that reading minds or stealing people's strength wasn't possible. So what was going on?

Luckily, Joe had offered to talk to me after the show and answer at least some of my questions, although he made sure I understood that he wouldn't be telling me any secrets. He agreed that he didn't really read my mind. He just made it seem like he did because he's a specific kind of magician, called a mentalist.

"I don't saw a person in half or walk through a plate of glass," he tells me. "I do magic that has to do with the mind—telepathy, precognition, clairvoyance, and psychokinesis."

I had to look all those words up. *Telepathy* is defined as mind reading and communicating using thoughts; *precognition* as predicting the future; *clairvoyance* as sensing things that we can't normally know using the five senses; and *psychokinesis* as the ability to move objects with your mind.

"Those are the four 'abilities' that would fall under the umbrella of mentalism," he continued. "Basically, I'm pretending to have the same abilities that psychics claim to have." A psychic is someone who says they can read minds or see ghosts or predict the future. In movies, they're often depicted wearing heavy purple robes, gazing into a crystal ball, or "reading" special cards (often those tarot cards we learned about earlier) to see what your future might have in store.

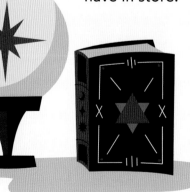

While psychics tell people that they actually have these special powers, there isn't any acceptable scientific evidence that these kinds of abilities really exist. What Joe did in his act was make me and the other audience members *think* that he had these powers. And while he wouldn't share the details of how he did that, I did get some explanations from a friend of his—Dr. Tony Barnhart. He's a professor of psychology, which is the science of how humans think and behave. Dr. Barnhart also used to be a professional magician, so he knows a thing or two about the world of magic— although he wouldn't tell me any secrets, either! He did share that the things that magicians do during their acts often involve psychology. Magicians also take advantage of how our attention spans work by utilizing something called misdirection.

"We can't process everything around us," Dr. Barnhart said. "So we have to decide what's important and what's not. What are we going to pay attention to, and what are we going to ignore? One of the ways we decide what to pay attention to is by watching what other people are paying attention to."

Here's an example: If you're in a group of people and someone starts looking in a different direction, there's a pretty good chance that you'll turn to see what they're looking at. Even babies do this! It's partially a social skill—we want to know what people around us are doing so we can be part of the group—and it's also a survival skill, because if another person spots danger, we will want to see it, too. Evolution has hardwired us to do this, and magicians know it. If they're trying to do a sleight of hand—a trick move that lets them maneuver cards or coins without you seeing—they want your attention fixed else- where. So they'll make sure they look in a different direction, and the audience will follow their gaze.

"If I look at my own hands while I'm carrying out a sleight of hand, the audience is going to look at my hands," said Dr. Barnhart. "In order to learn magic, you often have to learn the trick so well that it becomes automatic and you don't even need to look at what you're doing."

OK, that made sense to me—getting people to look over *there* while the magician does something over *here* seems pretty obvious, now that I think about it. But what about something like sawing a person in half? Dr. Barnhart tells me that magicians are using another type of misdirection there.

"Let's say you're out for a walk, and you see a dog behind a picket fence," he says. "You actually only see pieces of that dog, because you're looking at him through the pickets. But your brain automatically assumes that he's a complete dog behind that fence, and it fills in the missing pieces so that you are seeing a whole dog."

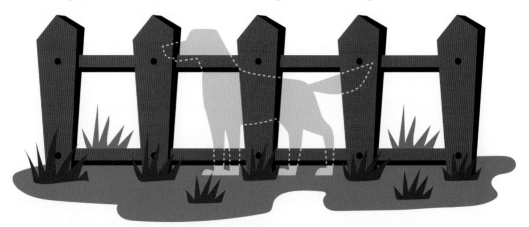

This, he tells me, is a process called good continuation. You only have pieces, but your brain makes things seem whole by filling in the gaps with the information that makes the most sense. In the trick where the magician saws a woman in half, the audience believes the feet sticking out of one side of the box and the head sticking out of the other are connected to the same person.

"The trick requires the audience to have good continuation," he says. "They can only see the head and feet, but they fill in the incomplete information about the woman in that box. And that's what you would normally assume, right? You've never seen a dog behind a picket fence and then walked behind the fence to find a bunch of slices of a dog!"

Nope! It's always a complete dog (or at least the dog in my neighbor's yard is always a complete dog). For the same reason the brain assumes that there's an entire dog behind that fence, it also assumes that there's an entire woman in that box on stage—that's how the trick is set up. (This is an old trick and not as much of a secret as other ones. If you want to know how the magician does the trick, you can go to the last page of this chapter and turn the book upside down—I've done this to keep from spilling a secret that you might not want to know!)

MAGIC AND SPIES

Hiding things in plain sight, carrying out sleights of hand, using misdirection, keeping secrets—all are techniques used successfully by magicians for hundreds of years. But there is another group of people for whom those tricks are useful: spies.

Maybe you've heard of the U.S. Central Intelligence Agency (CIA). This is an organization that collects information—also known as intelligence—on foreign countries so the U.S. government can make smart decisions that help keep Americans safe. Part of that intelligence gathering involves spying on certain people or countries. Spies need to be able to do their work—like accessing important documents or smuggling people out of another country—without getting caught. And who better to teach these kinds of techniques than a magician?

In 1953, the CIA hired John Mulholland, a professional magician, and paid him to write a top-secret manual that would teach some of his magic tricks to spies. The book had suggestions on how to use shoelaces to send messages (by tying them in different patterns) and how to sneak someone out of the country using secret compartments (like the kind that would be found in a magic act). It also talked about how spies could use sleight of hand to do something sneaky without being noticed, like dropping a pill in someone's drink while distracting them and making them look the other way. And it suggested hiding important notes or other small items inside everyday objects, such as matchbooks and toothpaste tubes, because those kinds of objects wouldn't attract attention.

The CIA supposedly destroyed all the copies of Mulholland's book in the 1970s, but at least one copy survived. Decades later, in 2009, two former intelligence officers republished *The Official C.I.A. Manual of Trickery and Deception*, which anyone—including you—can read.

I found these ideas about how to manipulate the way our brains work pretty fascinating. Then Dr. Barnhart told me about one more psychological trick that magicians use, and it has to do with memory and trust. He explained that most people do not have perfect memories—they don't remember everything that happens in perfect order, with perfect details. Our memories are what's called fallible, which means we easily make mistakes or are wrong about what we remember.

We humans also tend to trust one another, so when someone else remembers an event, we will often believe their memory, especially if ours isn't so clear. Magicians know this, so one of the things they'll do, Dr. Barnhart told me, is talk about the steps of a magic trick in a way that seems like they're reminding the audience of what happened. However, the magician might rearrange the order of events or change small details, which alters the audience's memory.

He asked me a question: "Is it a better trick if I give you a deck of cards, I let you shuffle that deck of cards, you take out a card, put it back in, and I find it? Or is it better if I give you a deck of cards, you take out the card, you put it back in, you shuffle the deck, you hand the deck back to me, and I find your card?"

I tell him the second one's better, because I get to shuffle the deck after I've put the card back in—I have more control over the cards.

"A magician will often do it the first way. They'll have you shuffle the deck; then they'll have you take a card and put it back in. But before they find the card, when they're talking to the audience about the trick, they'll say, 'Remember you took a card, you put it back in the deck, you shuffled that deck—and now I'm going to find your card, right?' All those things happened, just not in that order. But people will often adopt the magician's order of events, probably because we're trusting."

The magician gave us a lot of information in a very short period of time and then took advantage of how our attention spans and memories work, as well as our tendency to trust others. While I wasn't sure I liked the idea that someone could do this in normal life, it makes a magic show much more exciting and surprising.

"So was Joe Diamond doing the same kinds of things?" I asked Dr. Barnhart. "I mean, I don't think he can read minds, but it sure seemed like he was!"

Dr. Barnhart points out that mentalists (and psychics) tend to use our limited attention spans against us. "They make a lot of statements very quickly," he explains. "They know that your brain can't process everything they're saying, and you'll pick out the information that matters most to you, that fits with how you already see the world. And then you'll ignore all the other stuff that doesn't connect with that."

If someone tells us that they can read minds, we want to believe them. It's definitely fun (and maybe a little spooky) to go see a fortune teller or magician and have someone predict your future or guess what you're thinking, especially if they turn out to be right. But it's your brain that's choosing which information is correct, not the mind reader. That's the part we have to remember.

"The way our brains work can be used by others, both for good and for bad," says Dr. Barnhart. "But these tendencies are really important out in the real world. They help us make snap decisions. If you had to spend a lot of time thinking about that stuff, you wouldn't be able to respond to threats quickly."

For instance, what if you were riding your bike, thinking about what's for lunch, when all of a sudden, a lizard runs out in front of you. If you first had to tell your brain, *Brain! Quit thinking about grilled cheese sandwiches, and watch out for that lizard!*, you wouldn't have time to swerve or brake. But because your brain reacts automatically, you can avoid disaster. These automatic responses that we have—where our attention goes, how we filter out information, how our brain fills in gaps—all of these are behaviors that we've developed to help us survive and make quick decisions. We need them, and they're important to our daily lives, so it's not something we want to change about ourselves. But they're also the types of behavior that a magician can take advantage of, so it's good to be aware of them!

After watching Joe's show and talking to Dr. Barnhart, it was clear to me that science and stage magic definitely had some overlap. But even though I knew that these had been tricks, I'd still been pretty astonished by Joe's show. To be honest, a very small part of me hoped that maybe he did have some supernatural powers. Logically, and scientifically, I knew he probably didn't. And I knew that the other kinds of magic I'd looked into also had facts and science behind them. So why was the idea that there still might be some real magic—something mysterious or unknown—so appealing? Not just for me, but for lots of people? Why do we like the idea of magic?

WOMAN IN A BOX TRICK

There are two women in the box on stage—one has her head sticking out, the other her feet. But the audience sees only one woman get into the box. And, as an added bit of trickery, sometimes the magician uses a box that has the silhouette of a woman painted along the side of the box facing the audience—which also makes your brain think that there's only one woman in there.

MAGIC IS WONDERFUL

A funny thing happened the day I started writing this last chapter. It was a beautiful spring morning in mid-May, with big fluffy white clouds and a bright blue sky. The trees were leafing out and flowering, the tulips and lilacs were blooming. My cats rolled in the dirt and chased bugs, the air felt fresh—all I wanted to do was be outside, not at my desk. And as I stood staring out the window of my office (probably like you stare out the window at school on a beautiful day), guess what flew right past? A hummingbird! And then another one!

Whoa! I thought excitedly. *Did Cassie's spell finally work?*

It had been just about two months since Cassie and I met in her living room. While I'd been talking to all these people about magic and typing away at my computer, I just kept thinking about that spell. To be honest, I'd been feeling a little disappointed, because so far I hadn't seen hide nor hair nor feather nor beak of anything that might be considered a familiar. And, as you may remember, I was kinda holding out hope that it would be a hummingbird. So spotting not just one but two really did feel magical—knowing that they'd flown thousands and thousands of miles during their annual migration, seeing their tiny wings beat a million times a minute, watching them dart around and snack on the sugar water I'd made for them before they went zipping off into the sky.

However, I also knew that I needed to think sensibly about this. After all, it was spring, which is when the hummingbirds usually arrive in town each year. I'd put out feeders like I do every year, and hummingbirds remember from year to year where to find food. And it was really nice out, warm and sunny, so a good day for the birds to be out and about. Chances are that Cassie's spell had nothing to do with their appearance. But even though I knew there were perfectly rational and scientific reasons for those hummingbirds to arrive, a tiny part of me still liked the idea that her magic had worked. Why? Why did I want magic to be real?

Thinking back to all the conversations I'd had about this subject, I realized there were a couple of things about the idea of magic that I really liked. For one, magic is about having some control over the world around us. Dr. Stuart Vyse—the psychologist we met earlier who wrote a book about superstitions—pointed out that we don't actually have a lot of power over what happens in our day-to-day lives, good or bad. Because we can't make sure good things happen or prevent bad ones, we sometimes turn to ideas of magic. Imagine for a moment how great it would be if we could actually cast a spell to pass that test. Or prevent a pet from getting sick. Or bring an end to something scary like war or climate change. Of course we would use magic!

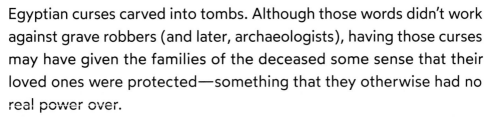

Lucky objects are a perfect example of this. For instance, I get kind of nervous when I fly, so I have a little orange fox on a keychain that I take with me to make sure everything goes smoothly. I don't think it's really keeping the plane in the air, but I've still rubbed its nose so much that the paint has come off. Or think about the ancient Egyptian curses carved into tombs. Although those words didn't work against grave robbers (and later, archaeologists), having those curses may have given the families of the deceased some sense that their loved ones were protected—something that they otherwise had no real power over.

Of course, not all magic is good (think of Voldemort, the Wicked Witch of the West, Vecna, Maleficent). There are curses, for instance, that could be called black magic—trying to use mysterious forces for evil or selfish purposes—like those curse tablets used by ancient Greeks and Romans, or the curse laid on poor Mr. Vance Vanders. Someone who wanted their rival to be unlucky in love or wanted revenge on someone might use magic to get their way. But what

I realized is that people who use black magic have the same basic motive as anyone else—they want to have some control.

Even Cassie told me that she uses magic in part because she wants to change the world—but unlike Voldemort, Cassie's goal is to make the world a better place. You might remember her talking about the idea of energy—the thoughts and feelings and actions that she puts into her magical practices, in the hopes that that energy will make good things happen.

"Energy is all around us," she said. "And since everything we do in this world affects everything else around us, the kind of energy we put in, good or bad, matters. We are all part of the universe, and we need to remember that we are all connected."

Cassie explained that she sees magic as another way she can try to do things that are beneficial for everyone, but also a way to feel like she's a part of the world. By putting energy out and paying attention to what happens next, and how her actions and thoughts affect others, she feels like she has a better understanding of how to connect. And that connection isn't just to people, either—it's to animals, plants, even rocks. It's trying to imagine that everything on this planet and in this universe is important and that you should treat it as such.

She pointed out that this is something humans aren't always good at. We like to think of ourselves as being separate from nature, she said, but we aren't. In Cassie's mind, magic is a way to make a stronger connection to the world and figure out how to best be a part of everything. To me, that sounded like a great reason to believe in magic.

And what she said reminded me of those strange artifacts from the Paleolithic that we learned about back in chapter 2. Remember that tusk carved out of mammoth ivory? With the head of a lion and the body of a human? While we don't know for sure what it symbolized, some anthropologists have inferred that it was a way for humans to try to create a magical connection with animals.

Or think about astrology—another example of how people have tried to create a sense of connection with the universe and nature. By watching the patterns of planets, constellations, and the moon, people came up with a system that they thought would help guide them and give them clues to the future, almost like getting advice from the sky. Feeling like they had that kind of relationship with the stars must have seemed pretty magical!

A sense of control, a way to try to do good things, a connection to the world around us, a love of nature—all of these explain why magic is so appealing. But the more I thought about it, the more I realized that there was something *else* that made me really like the idea of magic, and it is also one of the reasons I like science: They both make me more curious. If something feels somewhat mysterious and surprising, whether it's a mind-reading magician or lead turning into gold, it feels magical. And even if it turns out that there are rational, scientific reasons for why something happens, it still makes me want to know more—and it can still feel like magic, because it's so amazing.

I remembered back to something Dr. Gosden had told me—that magic is subjective, because it's based on personal feelings and beliefs rather than facts. It's a fact that the hummingbirds showed up in my yard. But along with that fact, I had feelings of excitement, happiness, amazement, and wonder.

Maybe it's those feelings that are the magic? I thought.

Wonder, especially, seemed important. Throughout history, the things we see in the world that we don't have a good explanation for make us wonder. Wonder gets us to ask questions, and questions are how we figure out the world. Think back to those philosophers in Ancient Greece who decided that the world was made of four elements. It's because they wondered how the world was put together. Likewise, the alchemists wondered if they could speed up the process of Earth's evolution and turn one metal into another. The ancient Egyptians and the Mesopotamians wondered why the sun, the moon, and the stars moved in certain ways, and if those movements had any effects on human life.

To wonder about something means to ask questions and to try to figure those questions out. Sometimes our hypotheses might be wrong. There's no scientific evidence that the stars have an effect on our personal lives or our futures. The idea that fire, water, earth, and air made up everything in the universe wasn't correct, and the alchemists' idea that you could turn lead into gold wasn't right, either. But we won't ever know things unless we ask questions, and we won't ask questions unless we are curious. Wondering is a very good starting point, because it eventually leads us to learn more about the world and ourselves.

What is the world made of? Why did the sun disappear like that? Why do we see that constellation of stars only some of the time? How do I protect my loved ones in the afterlife? How do I make my friend feel better? How might I improve my luck? Can I make animals (or people) do what I want? Learning always starts with a question—with that feeling of wondering. Another thing I realized is that wonder is at the heart of the scientific method that we learned about in the first chapter. The very first step in that set of directions that scientists use for their experiments is this: Ask a question—what are you wondering?

I spoke with Dr. Larry Hass, who is both a philosopher (like the ancient Greeks) and a magician, and he told me that imagination (which might include magical ideas) and curiosity are central to science. "Wonder comes first," he told me. "For instance, let's pretend we're our distant ancestors, and we see fire for the first time. We are like, 'Holy smokes! Look at that stuff over there! Where did that come from? Why does it do that?' And then later we might think, 'How can we create that fire ourselves?' So from wonder, we become interested in knowing more."

If you have something you're wondering about, you come up with a possible answer—a hypothesis. And it's important to note that, even if the answer is science and not magic (which it probably is), it doesn't make the world any less wondrous. For instance, I knew that Cassie's spell was supposed to bring me a familiar. When the hummingbirds arrived, there was a brief moment where it felt like the spell had worked. Plus, thinking back to what Cassie had said about energy,

I realized I had put energy into attracting them—providing food and a nice garden to hang out in—and now their energy was all around me as they zoomed around the yard and slurped up sugar water. Even when I admitted it was just the time of year that hummingbirds normally appear, it didn't make their appearance any less magical.

And as I pointed out in the beginning, science does seem a lot like magic. Think about spring: Plants that look dead come back to life. One day there are no flowers, and the next they're everywhere. Bees wallow in pollen and take it back to their hive, and it gets turned into honey. You put some tiny seeds in the ground, give them some water, and voilà! In a few months, they'll be giant, five-foot-tall sunflowers. Even though we know that science can explain what's happening and why, it still has a feel of magic to it.

I asked Dr. Hass one of the questions I'd been thinking about since the very beginning: Is it OK to be science-minded and also interested in magic?

"Science and magic are not opposed," he responded. "Wonder makes it possible to ask the question, which helps us be creative and imaginative when we come up with a hypothesis. And magic gives us the feeling that the world might be different than we thought. It gets us out of our ruts—our normal ways of looking at things. Magical ideas keep our curiosity in motion."

Of course, we have to keep those ideas in check. Yes, we have to be open-minded to all kinds of possibilities, but we can't be so open-minded that our brains fall out. I still don't think there is magic in the way that books and movies depict it, but I have learned that there are a lot of magical ideas that have some real science behind them, like curses and using herbal potions to heal the body.

Other practices like alchemy, although they seem magical now, came from a time when people didn't understand science as well as we do now but were still trying to find rational ways to explain the world. Our distant ancestors might have thought that the gods brought fire and that saying some sort of chant would let them control it. That was their hypothesis at the time, based on how they understood the world. Now, of course, we might look back on those ideas as magical thinking, but that's only because we have more information and a better understanding of the science behind what's happening.

But even though we have better tools and more technology than our ancestors, there is still a lot more to learn, and we can only make our best guesses about how the world works based on our current knowledge. As I said before, it could be that, in a thousand years, future humans will look back at how we tried to understand the universe and think that we were the ones practicing magic.

We don't have all the answers. We might not ever. And that's good, because mysteries and things that seem like magic keep us asking questions. Even when we do know the answers, it doesn't have to make what we're wondering about feel any less like magic. And it's that feeling of magic—of wonder, of curiosity, of possibility—that's magical in and of itself, even if there are no wands involved.

ALCHEMY AT HOME

Want to try a little alchemy of your own? Here's a fun and safe experiment to try at home (with the help of an adult). You'll need:

- **Small glass bowl or glass jar**

- **¼ cup white vinegar**

- **1 teaspoon salt**

- **25 pennies (make sure they're from before 1982—older pennies have more copper in them, which is useful for this experiment)**

- **Rubber glove**

- **Paper towel**

- **2 clean (not rusty or dirty) steel or iron nails**

INSTRUCTIONS

1. Pour the vinegar into the bowl or jar
2. Add salt and stir until it is dissolved.
3. Take a penny and submerge it into the vinegar solution halfway for 10 seconds.
4. Remove penny and observe—what do you notice?
5. Put all the pennies into the vinegar solution and let them sit for 10–15 minutes.
6. Wearing a glove, remove the pennies and put them on a paper towel.
7. Put one nail into the bowl and make sure it's fully covered with the solution. Let sit for 15–20 minutes.
8. Take the nail out and compare it to the other nail. Does it look different? If not, return the nail to the vinegar and continue to let it sit.

WHAT IS HAPPENING?

The vinegar is an acid and, along with the salt, it will strip some of the copper from the pennies. Those copper atoms remain in the vinegar-salt mixture. When you put the nail in the bowl, those copper atoms are attracted to the iron in the nail and attach to it, building up a layer of copper.

We know now that this is a chemical reaction, but were we to do this experiment hundreds of years ago, it would have seemed like the nails were changing from one type of metal to another—alchemy!

GLOSSARY

alchemy—The study of how to change common metals into more rare metals. People who study alchemy are known as alchemists.

amulet—An object that supposedly has special powers and can bring good luck.

anthropology—The study of humans, both past and present. Physical anthropology looks at how humans evolved from other animals and how they have adapted to their environments. Cultural anthropology looks at how people live, the rules they follow, and what values and ideas they consider important. Someone who studies anthropology is an anthropologist.

antibacterial—Something that works by killing bacteria or keeping it from growing.

archaeology—The study of humans that looks at the things they have left behind, like art and tools and pottery. Someone who studies archaeology is an archaeologist.

artifact—An object made by a human being from any time or place.

astrology—The study of the influence that the stars and planets may have on people's lives. Someone who studies astrology is an astrologer.

astronomy—The study of space. A scientist who studies astronomy is an astronomer.

atom—The smallest building blocks of matter.

belief—The idea that something is true but cannot be proven by science.

biological classification—A system used by scientists to describe living things.

binomial nomenclature—A system of naming plants and animals using two names: one for their genus and one for their species.

botany—The study of plants. Someone who studies botany is known as a botanist.

causation—When one event causes another event to occur.

chemical reaction—A process in which one or more chemicals are changed into other chemicals.

chemistry—The study of what things are made of and how these things interact with one another.

coincidence—An event that is not planned or arranged but seems like it is.

compound—A substance made up of different elements that are joined by a chemical bond.

concoction—A mixture of food or drinks that is made up of a variety of ingredients.

constellation—A group of stars that appear to form a pattern or shape when viewed from Earth.

correlation—When two events are related.

crystallization—A method in chemistry for transforming a liquid into a solid.

curse—A statement or wish that something bad will happen to someone.

distillation—A process in chemistry of separating out two or more liquids from a mixture.

Egyptologist—A scientist who studies Ancient Egypt.

element—A substance that contains only one kind of atom. They are the building blocks of everything in the universe, and they cannot be broken down into anything simpler.

The Enlightenment—Also known as the Age of Reason, this was a period in European history that began in the 1700s and focused on the use of reason and science to understand the natural world.

evaporation—A process in chemistry of turning a liquid into a gas.

hypothesis—An educated guess that can be tested by science.

inference—A conclusion reached using evidence and logic.

mass—The amount of matter an object contains.

matter—Anything that has mass and takes up space.

mentalist—A type of magician whose tricks focus on the mind.

Mesopotamia—An ancient region of the Middle East between the Tigris and Euphrates Rivers.

microbiology—The study of tiny organisms that are invisible to the eye, like bacteria and viruses. A scientist who studies microbiology is a microbiologist.

neurology—The study of the brain, spinal cord, and nerves. Someone who studies neurology is a neurologist.

nocebo effect—A situation in which a patient develops side effects or symptoms simply because the patient believes they may occur.

objective—A viewpoint that is based on facts without letting personal feelings get in the way.

Paleolithic—The earliest period of the Stone Age, which began about 2.7 million years ago.

periodic table—A system for arranging the chemical elements.

philosophy—The study of questions about truth, knowledge, humans, and the natural world. The word philosophy means "love of wisdom," and people who study philosophy are known as philosophers.

pictogram—A way of communicating information using images instead of words.

placebo—A treatment for a disease or condition that is meant not to work.

placebo effect—Treatments that should not have any result, but that somehow still make people feel better.

psychic—A person who claims to use supernatural powers to do things like read minds or find information that normal people cannot sense.

psychology—The scientific study of the ways that people think, feel, and behave. A scientist who studies psychology is a psychologist.

skepticism—A doubtful attitude about whether something exists or is true.

sleight of hand—A secret move or trick that lets magicians maneuver objects like cards or coins without the audience seeing.

subatomic—Particles that are smaller than an atom, such as protons, neutrons, and electrons.

subjective—A viewpoint that is based on personal feelings and beliefs rather than facts.

sublimation—A process in chemistry where a solid substance changes into a gas without first becoming a liquid.

Vodou—A type of religion that began centuries ago in West Africa and was later brought to the Americas by African people who had been forced into slavery. The word *Vodou* means "spirit" in a West African language known as Fon.

zodiac—A belt of space around Earth.

NOTES

INTRODUCTION: **I PUT A SPELL ON YOU**

2   Familiar: Suzannah Lipscomb, *A History of Magic, Witchcraft, and the Occult.* New York: DK Publishing (2020), p. 187.

3   Spin of the Earth: See Ibrahim Sawal, "How Fast Does Earth Spin?" *New Scientist*; www.newscientist.com/question/fast-earth-spin.

CHAPTER 1: **SCIENCE VS. MAGIC**

13   Lead into gold: See John Matson, "Fact or Fiction? Lead Can Be Turned into Gold." *Scientific American*, January 31, 2014; www. scientificamerican.com/article/fact-or-fiction-lead-can-be-turned-into-gold.

13   1941: See William Laurence, "Mercury Smashed Into 'Radium-Gold.'" *New York Times*, May 3, 1941; timesmachine.nytimes .com/timesmachine/1941/05/03/88099521.html?pdf_redirect =true&ip=0&pageNumber=17.

13   Alchemy as silly: See *Mysteries of the Unknown: Secrets of the Alchemists.* New York: Time-Life Books (1990), p. 136.

15   Scientific method: See "Steps of the Scientific Method." Science Buddies; www.sciencebuddies.org/science-fair-projects/science-fair/ steps-of-the-scientific-method.

17   Gosden, Chris. *Magic: A History: From Alchemy to Witchcraft, from the Ice Age to the Present.* New York: Picador, 2020.

CHAPTER 2: **A (BRIEF) MAGICAL HISTORY**

26   Hunting magic: See "Hunting Magic in Rock Art." Bradshaw Foundation, December 9, 2019; bradshawfoundation.com/news/rock_art. php?id=Hunting-magic-in-rock-art.

26 Cave art: Ian Tattersall, *Masters of the Planet: The Search for Our Human Origins.* New York: St. Martin's Press (2012), p. xv.

27 History of writing: See Ewan Clayton, "Where Did Writing Begin?" British Library; www.bl.uk/history-of-writing/articles/where-did-writing begin.

27 Kish tablets: See en.wikipedia.org/wiki/Kish_tablet.

29 Zodiac explainer: See *Britannica Kids*, kids.britannica.com/students/article/astrology/272987.

29 Zodiac signs: See Kristen Bobst, "How to Understand Zodiac Signs Through the Stars." *Treehugger*, May 30, 2020; www.treehugger.com/how-understand-zodiac-signs-through-stars-4863741.

30 Constellations: See "What Are Constellations?" NASA Science Space Place, updated December 6, 2022; spaceplace.nasa.gov/constellations/en.

30 Zodiac shift: See Danny Lewis, "NASA Didn't Change Your Astrological Star Sign, Blame It on Earth's Wobbly Rotation." *Smithsonian Magazine*, September 26, 2016; www.smithsonianmag.com/smart-news/nasa-didnt-change-your-astrological-sign-stars-did-180960584.

31 Astrology and science: See Stephen Luntz, "How We Know Astrology Isn't Real." *IFLScience*, March 24, 2023; www.iflscience.com/how-we-know-astrology-isnt-real-68150.

32 Mesopotamia healers: See Joshua Mark, "Medicine in Ancient Mesopotamia." World History Encyclopedia, January 25, 2023; www.worldhistory.org/article/687/medicine-in-ancient-mesopotamia.

33 Egyptian healers: See Susan Okie, "Egyptian Physicians—Healers from 1500 BC Were Surprisingly Ahead of Their Time." *Tampa Bay Times*, updated October 16, 2005; www.tampabay.com/archive/1990/01/21/egyptian-physicians-healers-from-1500-b-c-were-surprisingly-ahead-of-their-time.

33 "Ebers papyrus": See *Encyclopedia Britannica*, www.britannica.com/topic/Ebers-papyrus.

34 Curse tablets: See Greg Woolf, "Curse Tablets: The History of a Technology." *Greece & Rome*, vol. 69, special issue 1 (New York: Cambridge University Press, April 2022, pp. 120–34); www.cambridge.org/core/journals/greece-and-rome/article/curse-tablets-the-history-of-a-technology/FC52B9C97B9ED7D34405D8DD1A4A3B2A.

34 Wrapped around herbs or hair: See Alexandra Sofroniew, "An Ancient Curse Revealed." Getty, December 12, 2012; blogs.getty.edu/iris/an-ancient-curse-revealed.

34 Stolen clothes: See Carly Silver, "When Ancient Romans Had Their Clothes Stolen, They Responded with Curse Tablets." *Atlas Obscura*, August 9, 2016; www.atlasobscura.com/articles/when-ancient-romans-had-their-clothes-stolen-they-responded-with-curse-tablets.

35 Oracle at Delphi: See "The Oracle at Delphi." PBS.org, www.pbs.org/empires/thegreeks/background/7_p1.html.

36 Tarot: See "Tarot," www.britannica.com/topic/tarot.

36 History of tarot: See Patti Wigington, "A Brief History of Tarot." *Learn Religions*, June 6, 2018; www.learnreligions.com/a-brief-history-of-tarot-2562770.

39 Punishment for magic: See Michael D. Bailey, *Magic: The Basics*. New York: Routledge (2018), pp. 72–5.

CHAPTER 3: **FROM LEAD INTO GOLD**

46 Alchemy overview: See John A. Stewart, "A Brief History of Alchemy." Johnastewart.org, February 1, 2017; johnastewart.org/networked-narratives/a-brief-history-of-alchemy.

47 The Greek Elements: See "Aristotle," chemed.chem.purdue.edu/genchem/history/aristotle.html.

49 Six emperors: See Amelia Soth, "Elixirs of Immortal Life Were a Deadly Obsession." *JSTOR Daily*, December 28, 2018; daily.jstor.org/elixir-immortal-life-deadly-obsessions.

49 Gunpowder: See Amanda Yarnell, "History's Hidden Fire." *Chemical & Engineering News*, January 17, 2005; cen.acs.org/articles/83/i3/Historys-Hidden-Fire.html.

50 Fireworks: See Alex Knapp, "This Fourth of July, Stop to Thank Chinese Alchemists." *Forbes*, July 4, 2014; www.forbes.com/sites/alexknapp/2014/07/04/this-fourth-of-july-stop-to-thank-chinese-alchemists/?sh=3b383f8c2d47.

50 Alchemy: Chris Gosden, *Magic: A History: From Alchemy to Witchcraft, from the Ice Age to the Present.* New York: Picador (2020), pp. 370–73.

50 Jābir ibn Hayyān: See Ayomide Akinbode, "How Jabir Ibn Haiyan became the Father of Modern Chemistry." The Historyville, July 27, 2020; www.thehistoryville.com/jabir-ibn-hayyan.

52 Elements: See Anne Marie Helmenstine, "How Many Elements Can Be Found Naturally?" Thought Co., updated September 1, 2019; www.thoughtco.com/how-many-elements-found-naturally-606636.

52 Foundations of chemistry: See Reshma Kolala, "The Roots of Chemistry: How the Ancient Tradition of Alchemy Influenced Modern Scientific Thought." Aggie Transcript, May 8, 2020; aggietranscript.ucdavis.edu/the-roots-of-chemistry-how-the-ancient-tradition-of-alchemy-influenced-modern-scientific-thought.

53 Periodic Table: See National Center for Biotechnology Information. "Periodic Table of Elements." PubChem, pubchem.ncbi.nlm.nih.gov/periodic-table.

55 Alchemists' codes: See "Uncover the Reason Why the Alchemist's Attempted to Conceal Their Chemical Knowledge and How." *Britannica*, www.britannica.com/video/187015/alchemists-knowledge.

55 Alchemy history: See "Alchemy, Aristotle and Alchemists." University of Hawaii, www.honolulu.hawaii.edu/instruct/natsci/science/brill/sci122/TVtext/23/MOD23.htm#.

58 Magical view of alchemy: See *Mysteries of the Unknown: Secrets of the Alchemists.* New York: Time-Life Books (1990), p. 136.

CHAPTER 4: **DRINK ME**

63 Shakespeare, William. *Macbeth.* Act 4, Scene 1.

65 Binomial nomenclature: See "Binomial nomenclature," Biology Online, www.biologyonline.com/dictionary/binomial-nomenclature.

66 Biological classification: See "Biological classification," *Britannica Kids*, kids.britannica.com/students/article/biological-classification/611149.

67 Dandelion: See en.wikipedia.org/wiki/Taraxacum_officinale.

68 Multiple flowers: See "Dandelion," Invasive.org, www.invasive.org/browse/subinfo.cfm?sub=3887.

68 Dragon's teeth: See "Lotus tetragonolobus," The Seed Site, theseedsite.co.uk/profile192.html.

68 Knotweed: See "Japanese Knotweed Benefits: How to Use the Knotweed Plant." MasterClass, March 22, 2022; www.masterclass.com/articles/japanese-knotweed-benefits.

68 Frog cheese: See "Bovista." DailyMed, (U.S. National Library of Medicine), updated June 18, 2015; dailymed.nlm.nih.gov/dailymed/drugInfo.cfm?setid=18c70ca5-56cc-1978-e054-00144ff8d46c.

69 Plants evolution: See Elizabeth Pennisi, "Land Plants Arose Earlier than Thought—and May Have Had a Bigger Impact on the Evolution of Animals." *Science*, February 19, 2018; www.science.org/content/article/land-plants-arose-earlier-thought-and-may-have-had-bigger-impact-evolution-animals.

69 Human evolution: See "What Does It Mean to Be Human?" Smithsonian National Museum of Natural History, updated January

22, 2021; humanorigins.si.edu/evidence/human-fossils/species/
homo-sapiens#.

70 History of herbalism: See "Herbal History: Roots of Western Herbalism,"
Herbal Academy, theherbalacademy.com/herbal-history.

70 Comfrey: See Christiane Staiger, "Comfrey Root: From Tradition to
Modern Clinical Trials." *Wiener medizinische Wochenschrift* (1946)
vol. 163, 3–4 (2013): 58–64 (doi:10.1007/s10354-012-0162-4);
www.ncbi.nlm.nih.gov/pmc/articles/PMC3580139.

70 Elderberry: See Evelin Tiralongo, et al., "Elderberry Supplementation
Reduces Cold Duration and Symptoms in Air-Travellers: A Randomized,
Double-Blind Placebo-Controlled Clinical Trial." *Nutrients*, vol. 8,
March 2016 (doi:10.3390/nu8040182); www.ncbi.nlm.nih.gov/
pmc/articles/PMC4848651.

71 Paleolithic medicine: See Karen Hardy, "Paleomedicine and the
Evolutionary Context of Medicinal Plant Use." *Revista Brasiliera
de Farmacognosia*, vol. 31, pp. 1–15 (2021); link.springer.com/
article/10.1007/s43450-020-00107-4.

74 Goblin potion: See "Bald's Leechbook," British Library, www.bl.uk/
collection-items/balds-leechbook.

74 Bald's Eyesalve: See Clare Wilson, "Anglo-Saxon Remedy Kills Hospital
Superbug MRSA." *New Scientist*, March 30, 2015; www.newscientist.
com/article/dn27263-anglo-saxon-remedy-kills-hospital-superbug-
mrsa.

74 Malaria drug: See Katie Hunt and Shen Lu, "Nobel Prize Winner
Tu Youyou Combed Ancient Chinese Texts for Malaria Cure." CNN,
updated October 6, 2015; www.cnn.com/2015/10/06/asia/china-
malaria-nobel-prize-tu-youyou/index.html.

75 Nobel Prize: See Celia Hatton, "Nobel Prize Winner Tu Youyou Helped
by Ancient Chinese Remedy." BBC, October 6, 2015; www.bbc.com/
news/blogs-china-blog-34451386.

75 Snake oil history: See Lakshmi Gandhi, "A History of 'Snake Oil Salesmen.'" *NPR Code Switch*, August 26, 2013; www.npr.org/sections/codeswitch/2013/08/26/215761377/a-history-of-snake-oil-salesmen.

76 Ginger: See "Ginger," www.mountsinai.org/health-library/herb/ginger.

76 Licorice root: See Cristina Fiore, et al., "A History of the Therapeutic Use of Liquorice in Europe." *Journal of Ethnopharmacology*, vol. 99 (2005); www.ncbi.nlm.nih.gov/pmc/articles/PMC7125727.

77 Rue: See Rebecca Brackmann, "'It Will Help Him Wonderfully': Placebo and Meaning Responses in Early Medieval English Medicine." *Speculum: A Journal of Medieval Studies*, vol. 97, no. 4 (October 2022); www.journals.uchicago.edu/doi/full/10.1086/721680.

77 Placebo history: See Thea Baldrick, "The Surprisingly Advanced Medicine of Ancient Egypt." *The Collector*, April 2, 2022; www.thecollector.com/ancient-egyptian-medicine.

77 Placebo overview: See "Placebo," *Psychology Today*, www.psychologytoday.com/us/basics/placebo.

CHAPTER 5: **CURSES!**

82 Origin of the word *curse*: See "Curse," Online Etymology Dictionary, www.etymonline.com/word/curse.

82 Harry Potter curses: See "Unforgivable Curses," Harry Potter Wiki, harrypotter.fandom.com/wiki/Unforgivable_Curses.

83 Hope Diamond: See Richard Kurin, *Hope Diamond: The Legendary History of a Cursed Gem*. New York: HarperCollins (2006), p. 364.

83 The Bed of Ware: See "The Great Bed of Ware," *Atlas Obscura*, www.atlasobscura.com/places/the-great-bed-of-ware-london-england.

84 The Crying Boy: Robert Bartholomew and Benjamin Radford, *The Martians Have Landed! A History of Media-Driven Panics and Hoaxes*. Jefferson, NC: McFarland & Company (2011), p. 140.

86 Petety: Zahi Hawass, *Curse of the Pharaohs: My Adventures with Mummies*. New York: National Geographic Children's Books (2004), p. 45–7.

87 King Tut overview: See "King Tut," *National Geographic Education*, education.nationalgeographic.org/resource/king-tut.

87 Hussein Hassan Abdel Rassuhl: See Sara Ahmed, "The Egyptian Hero Behind Tutankhamun's Tomb Discovery." *Egyptian Streets*, July 13, 2018; egyptianstreets.com/2018/07/13/the-egyptian-hero-behind-tutankhamuns-tomb-discovery.

88 King Tut's curse: See Dave Kindy, "King Tut's Tomb Was Discovered 100 Years Ago—and Unleashed a 'Curse.'" *Washington Post*, November 4, 2022; www.washingtonpost.com/history/2022/11/04/king-tut-tomb-curse.

89 Causation: See "Thinking Critically About Experiments: Correlation vs. Causation." Kids Boost Immunity, updated November 30, 2022; kidsboostimmunity.com/thinking-critically-about-experiments-correlation-vs-causation-8.

89 Correlation: See Allan Bond, "Data Science for Kids—Correlation vs. Causation," Medium: Machine Learning, medium.com/mlearning-ai/data-science-for-kids-correlation-vs-causation-20fc8f7e5d9c.

90 Science of the mummy's curse: See Allison C. Meier, "Was It Really a Mummy's Curse?" *JSTOR Daily*, August 22, 2019; daily.jstor.org/was-it-really-a-mummys-curse.

90 Vanders case: Clifton K. Meader, *Symptoms of Unknown Origin: A Medical Odyssey*. Nashville, TN: Vanderbilt University Press (2005), pp. 27–32.

91 Vodou overview: *See Britannica Kids*, kids.britannica.com/students/article/Vodou/277629.

92 Magic words: Claude Lecouteux, *Dictionary of Ancient Magic Words and Spells: From Abraxas to Zoar.* New York: Simon & Schuster (2015), p. 8.

94 Nocebo: See David Robson, "The Contagious Thought That Could Kill You." BBC, February 10, 2015; www.bbc.com/future/article/20150210-can-you-think-yourself-to-death.

CHAPTER 6: KNOCK ON WOOD

99 Bless you: See Judy Mandell, "Why We Feel Compelled to Say 'Bless You' When Someone Sneezes." *New York Times*, September 17, 2019; www.nytimes.com/2019/09/17/well/mind/sneezing-sneezes-god-bless-you-manners-etiquette.html,

101 Broken mirrors: See Barry Markovsky, "How Did the Superstition That Broken Mirrors Cause Bad Luck Start and Why Does It Still Exist?" The Conversation, June 29, 2021; theconversation.com/how-did-the-superstition-that-broken-mirrors-cause-bad-luck-start-and-why-does-it-still-exist-162889.

101 Western superstitions: Stuart Vyse, *Superstition: A Very Short Introduction.* New York: Oxford University Press (2019), 78–81.

102 Evolution of superstition: See Kevin R. Foster and Hanna Kokko, "The Evolution of Superstitious and Superstition-Like Behaviour." *Proceedings of the Royal Society B: Biological Sciences*, vol. 276,1654 (2009), pp. 31–7; www.ncbi.nlm.nih.gov/pmc/articles/PMC2615824.

103 Seeking out patterns: See Michael Shermer, "Patternicity." *Scientific American*, December 2008, vol. 299, issue 6, p. 48.

104 Lucky object experiment: Lysann Damisch, Barbara Stoberock and Thomas Mussweiler, "Keep Your Fingers Crossed! How Superstition

Improves Performance." *Psychological Science*, vol. 21, no. 7, July 2010; www.jstor.org/stable/41062460.

105 Sports superstitions: See Robert Duff, "7 Most Famous Sports Superstitions." SportsBettingDime.com, March 5, 2021; www.sportsbettingdime.com/guides/articles/famous-sports-superstitions.

106 Peanuts: See Barbara Mikkelson, "NASCAR Peanuts Superstition." Snopes.com, March 7, 2010; www.snopes.com/fact-check/nascar-peanuts-superstition.

106 Mustache: See Chris Chase, "Why Was This Female Gold Medalist Sporting a Painted Mustache?" *USA Today*, February 16, 2014; ftw.usatoday.com/2014/02/mustache-snowboard-cross-eva-samkova.

CHAPTER 7: I KNOW WHAT YOU'RE THINKING

114 Magician's Oath: See "What Is the Magician's Oath and Why Is It Important." DailyHistory.org, dailyhistory.org/What_is_the_Magician%27s_Oath_and_why_is_it_important.

120 Mulholland: See "Secrets from the CIA Spy Manual of Trickery and Deception," Spyscape.com, spyscape.com/article/shocking-secrets-from-the-cia-spy-manual-of-trickery-and-deception.

125 Sawing women in half: Stephen L. Macknik and Susana Martinez-Conde, *Sleights of Mind: What the Neuroscience of Magic Reveals About Our Everyday Deceptions*. New York: Henry Holt and Company (2010), pp. 39–40.

ALCHEMY AT HOME

136 Experiment: See "Copper-plated nail," California State University of Bakersfield Department of Chemistry, www.csub.edu/chemistry/_files/copper%20plated%20nailAO.pdf.

BIBLIOGRAPHY

BOOKS

Bailey, Michael D. *Magic: The Basics*. New York: Routledge, 2018.

Barthlolomew, Robert and Benjamin Radford. *The Martians Have Landed! A History of Media-Driven Panics and Hoaxes*. Jefferson, NC: McFarland & Company, 2011.

Gosden, Chris. *Magic: A History: From Alchemy to Witchcraft, from the Ice Age to the Present*. New York: Picador, 2020.

Hawass, Zahi. *Curse of the Pharaohs: My Adventures with Mummies*. New York: National Geographic Society, 2004.

Kurin, Richard. *Hope Diamond: The Legendary History of a Cursed Gem*. New York: HarperCollins, 2006.

Lecouteux, Claude. *Dictionary of Ancient Magic Words and Spells: From Abraxas to Zoar*. New York: Simon & Schuster, 2015.

Lipscomb, Suzannah. *A History of Magic, Witchcraft, and the Occult*. New York: DK Publishing, 2020.

Macknik, Stephen L. and Susana Martinez-Conde. *Sleights of Mind: What the Neuroscience of Magic Reveals About Our Everyday Deceptions*. New York: Henry Holt and Company, 2010.

Meader, Clifton K. *Symptoms of Unknown Origin: A Medical Odyssey*. Nashville, TN: Vanderbilt University Press, 2005.

Tattersall, Ian. *Masters of the Planet: The Search for Our Human Origins.* New York: St. Martin's Press, 2012.

Time-Life Books. *Mysteries of the Unknown: Secrets of the Alchemists.* New York: Time-Life Books, 1990.

Vyse, Stuart. *Believing in Magic.* New York: Oxford University Press, 2014.

———. *Superstition: A Very Short Introduction.* New York: Oxford University Press, 2019.

JOURNALS

Brackmann, Rebecca. "'It Will Help Him Wonderfully': Placebo and Meaning Responses in Early Medieval English Medicine." *Speculum: A Journal of Medieval Studies*, vol. 97, no. 4, October 2022. See www.journals. uchicago.edu/doi/full/10.1086/721680.

Damisch, Lysann, Barbara Stoberock and Thomas Mussweiler. "Keep Your Fingers Crossed! How Superstition Improves Performance." *Psychological Science*, vol. 21, no. 7, July 2010. See www.jstor.org/stable/41062460.

Fiore, Cristina, et al. "A History of the Therapeutic Use of Liquorice in Europe." *Journal of Ethnopharmacology*, vol. 99 (2005), pp. 317–24. See www.ncbi.nlm.nih.gov/pmc/articles/PMC7125727.

Foster, Kevin R., and Hanna Kokko. "The Evolution of Superstitious and Superstition-Like Behaviour." *Proceedings of the Royal Society B: Biological Sciences*, vol. 276,1654 (2009). See www.ncbi.nlm.nih.gov/pmc/articles/PMC2615824.

Staiger, Christiane. "Comfrey Root: From Tradition to Modern Clinical Trials." *Wiener medizinische Wochenschrift* (1946), vol. 163, 3–4 (2013), pp. 58–64 (doi:10.1007/s10354-012-0162-4). See www.ncbi.nlm.nih.gov/pmc/articles/PMC3580139.

Tiralongo, Evelin, et al. "Elderberry Supplementation Reduces Cold Duration and Symptoms in Air-Travellers: A Randomized, Double-Blind

Placebo-Controlled Clinical Trial." *Nutrients*, vol. 8, March 2016 (doi:10.3390/nu8040182). See www.ncbi.nlm.nih.gov/pmc/articles/PMC4848651.

Woolf, Greg. "Curse Tablets: The History of a Technology." *Greece & Rome*, vol. 69, special issue 1 (New York: Cambridge University Press, April 2022). See www.cambridge.org/core/journals/greece-and-rome/article/curse-tablets-the-history-of-a-technology/FC52B9C97B9ED7D34405D8DD1A4A3B2A.

PLAYS

Shakespeare, William. *Macbeth*. Act IV, scene 1.

PERIODICALS

Laurence, William. "Mercury Smashed Into 'Radium-Gold.'" *New York Times*, May 3, 1941. See timesmachine.nytimes.com/timesmachine/1941/05/03/88099521.html?pdf_redirect=true&ip=0&pageNumber=17.

Lewis, Danny. "NASA Didn't Change Your Astrological Star Sign, Blame It on Earth's Wobbly Rotation." *Smithsonian Magazine*, September 26, 2016. See www.smithsonianmag.com/smart-news/nasa-didnt-change-your-astrological-sign-stars-did-180960584.

Mandell, Judy. "Why We Feel Compelled to Say 'Bless You' When Someone Sneezes." *New York Times*, September 17, 2019. See www.nytimes.com/2019/09/17/well/mind/sneezing-sneezes-god-bless-you-manners-etiquette.html.

Matson, John. "Fact or Fiction? Lead Can Be Turned into Gold." *Scientific American*, January 31, 2014. See www.scientificamerican.com/article/fact-or-fiction-lead-can-be-turned-into-gold.

Okie, Susan. "Egyptian Physicians—Healers from 1500 BC Were Surprisingly Ahead of Their Time." *Tampa Bay Times*, updated

October 16, 2005. See www.tampabay.com/archive/1990/01/21/
egyptian-physicians-healers-from-1500-b-c-were-surprisingly-
ahead-of-their-time.

Shermer, Michael. "Patternicity." *Scientific American*, vol. 299, issue 6,
December 2008.

WEBSITES

Ahmed, Sara. "The Egyptian Hero Behind Tutankhamun's Tomb
Discovery." Egyptian Streets, July 13, 2018. See egyptianstreets.
com/2018/07/13/the-egyptian-hero-behind-tutankhamuns-tomb-
discovery.

Akinbode, Ayomide. "How Jabir Ibn Haiyan became the Father of Modern
Chemistry." The Historyville, July 27, 2020. See www.thehistoryville.
com/jabir-ibn-hayyan.

"Alchemy, Aristotle and Alchemists." University of Hawaii. See www.
honolulu.hawaii.edu/instruct/natsci/science/brill/sci122/
TVtext/23/MOD23.htm#.

"Aristotle." See chemed.chem.purdue.edu/genchem/history/aristotle.
html.

Baird, Christopher S. "Can Gold Be Created from Other Elements?"
Science Questions with Surprising Answers, May 2, 2014. See
www.wtamu.edu/~cbaird/sq/2014/05/02/can-gold-be-created-
from-other-elements.

Baldrick, Thea. "The Surprisingly Advanced Medicine of Ancient Egypt."
The Collector, April 2, 2022. See www.thecollector.com/ancient-
egyptian-medicine.

"Binomial nomenclature." Biology Online. See www.biologyonline.com/
dictionary/binomial-nomenclature.

"Biological classification." *Britannica Kids*. See kids.britannica.com/
students/article/biological-classification/61114.

Bobst, Kristen. "How to Understand Zodiac Signs Through the Stars." Treehugger, May 30, 2020. See www.treehugger.com/how-understand-zodiac-signs-through-stars-4863741.

Bond, Allan. "Data Science for Kids—Correlation vs. Causation." Medium: Machine Learning. See medium.com/mlearning-ai/data-science-for-kids-correlation-vs-causation-20fc8f7e5d9c.

"Bovista." DailyMed (U.S. National Library of Medicine), updated June 18, 2015. See dailymed.nlm.nih.gov/dailymed/drugInfo.cfm?setid=18c70ca5-56cc-1978-e054-00144ff8d46c.

Chase, Chris. "Why Was This Female Gold Medalist Sporting a Painted Mustache?" USA Today, February 16, 2014. See ftw.usatoday.com/2014/02/mustache-snowboard-cross-eva-samkova.

Clayton, Ewan. "Where Did Writing Begin?" British Library. See www.bl.uk/history-of-writing/articles/where-did-writing-begin.

"Copper-plated nail." California State University of Bakersfield Department of Chemistry. See www.csub.edu/chemistry/_files/copper%20plated%20nailAO.pdf.

"Curse." Online Etymology Dictionary. See www.etymonline.com/word/curse.

"Dandelion." Invasive.org. See www.invasive.org/browse/subinfo.cfm?sub=3887.

"Ebers papyrus." Britannica.com. See www.britannica.com/topic/Ebers-papyrus.

Duff, Robert. "7 Most Famous Sports Superstitions." SportsBettingDime.com. March 5, 2021. See www.sportsbettingdime.com/guides/articles/famous-sports-superstitions.

Gandhi, Lakshmi. "A History of 'Snake Oil Salesmen.'" NPR Code Switch, August 26, 2013. See www.npr.org/sections/codeswitch/2013/08/26/215761377/a-history-of-snake-oil-salesmen.

"Ginger." Mount Sinai. See www.mountsinai.org/health-library/herb/ginger.

"The Great Bed of Ware." *Atlas Obscura.* See www.atlasobscura.com/places/the-great-bed-of-ware-london-england.

Hardy, Karen. "Paleomedicine and the Evolutionary Context of Medicinal Plant Use." *Revista Brasiliera de Farmacognosia* 31, 1–15 (2021). See link.springer.com/article/10.1007/s43450-020-00107-4.

Hatton, Celia. "Nobel Prize winner Tu Youyou helped by Ancient Chinese Remedy." BBC.com, October 6, 2015. See www.bbc.com/news/blogs-china-blog-34451386.

Helmenstine, Anne Marie. "How Many Elements Can Be Found Naturally?" Thought Co., updated Sept. 1, 2019. See www.thoughtco.com/how-many-elements-found-naturally-606636.

"Herbal History: Roots of Western Herbalism." Herbal Academy. See theherbalacademy.com/herbal-history.

Hunt, Katie and Shen Lu. "Nobel Prize Winner Tu Youyou Combed Ancient Chinese Texts for Malaria Cure." CNN.com, updated October 6, 2015. See www.cnn.com/2015/10/06/asia/china-malaria-nobel-prize-tu-youyou/index.html.

"Hunting magic," "Hunting magic in rock art." Bradshaw Foundation, December 9, 2019. See www.bradshawfoundation.com/news/rock_art.php?id=Hunting-magic-in-rock-art.

Kindy, Dave. "King Tut's Tomb Was Discovered 100 Years Ago—and Unleashed a 'Curse.'" *Washington Post*, November 4, 2022. See www.washingtonpost.com/history/2022/11/04/king-tut-tomb-curse.

"King Tut." *National Geographic Education*, education.nationalgeographic.org/resource/king-tut.

"Kish tablets." See en.wikipedia.org/wiki/Kish_tablet.

Knapp, Alex. "This Fourth of July, Stop to Thank Chinese Alchemists." *Forbes,* July 4, 2014. See www.forbes.com/sites/alexknapp/2014/07/04/this-fourth-of-july-stop-to-thank-chinese-alchemists/?sh=3b383f8c2d47.

Kolala, Reshma. "The Roots of Chemistry: How the Ancient Tradition of Alchemy Influenced Modern Scientific Thought." *Aggie Transcript*, May 8, 2020. See aggietranscript.ucdavis.edu/the-roots-of-chemistry-how-the-ancient-tradition-of-alchemy.

Mikkelson, Barbara. "NASCAR Peanuts Superstition." Snopes.com, March 7, 2010. See www.snopes.com/fact-check/nascar-peanuts-superstition.

Mount, Toni. "Snail Poultices and Blood Potions: 9 Weird Medieval Medicines." History Extra, April 20, 2015. See www.historyextra.com/period/medieval/9-weird-medieval-medicines.

National Center for Biotechnology Information. "Periodic Table of Elements." PubChem. See pubchem.ncbi.nlm.nih.gov/periodic-table.

"The Oracle at Delphi." PBS.org. See www.pbs.org/empires/thegreeks/background/7_p1.html.

Pennisi, Elizabeth. "Land Plants Arose Earlier Than Thought—And May Have Had a Bigger Impact on the Evolution of Animals." *Science*, February 19, 2018. See www.science.org/content/article/land-plants-arose-earlier-thought-and-may-have-had-bigger-impact-evolution-animals.

"Placebo." *Psychology Today*. See www.psychologytoday.com/us/basics/placebo.

Robson, David. "The Contagious Thought That Could Kill You." BBC.com, February 10, 2015. See www.bbc.com/future/article/20150210-can-you-think-yourself-to-death.

Sawal, Ibrahim. "How Fast Does Earth Spin?" *New Scientist*. See www.newscientist.com/question/fast-earth-spin.

"Secrets From the CIA Spy Manual of Trickery and Deception." Spyscape.com. See spyscape.com/article/shocking-secrets-from-the-cia-spy-manual-of-trickery-and-deception.

Silver, Carly. "When Ancient Romans Had Their Clothes Stolen, They Responded with Curse Tablets." *Atlas Obscura*, August 9, 2016.

See www.atlasobscura.com/articles/when-ancient-romans-had-their-clothes-stolen-they-responded-with-curse-tablets.

Stewart, John A. "A Brief History of Alchemy." Johnastewart.org, February 1, 2017. See johnastewart.org/networked-narratives/a-brief-history-of-alchemy.

Sofroniew, Alexandra. "An Ancient Curse Revealed." Getty, December 12, 2012. See blogs.getty.edu/iris/an-ancient-curse-revealed.

Soth, Amelia. "Elixirs of Immortal Life Were a Deadly Obsession." *JSTOR Daily*, December 28, 2018. See daily.jstor.org/elixir-immortal-life-deadly-obsessions.

"Steps of the Scientific Method." Science Buddies. See www.sciencebuddies.org/science-fair-projects/science-fair/steps-of-the-scientific-method.

"Tarot." See www.britannica.com/topic/tarot.

"Thinking Critically About Experiments: Correlation vs. Causation," Kids Boost Immunity, updated November 30, 2022. See kidsboostimmunity.com/thinking-critically-about-experiments-correlation-vs-causation-8.

"Uncover the Reason Why the Alchemist's Attempted to Conceal Their Chemical Knowledge and How." *Britannica*. See www.britannica.com/video/187015/alchemists-knowledge.

"Unforgivable Curses." Harry Potter Wiki. See harrypotter.fandom.com/wiki/Unforgivable_Curses.

"Vodou." *Britannica Kids*. See kids.britannica.com/students/article/Vodou/277629.

"What Are Constellations?" NASA Science Space Place, updated December 6, 2022. See spaceplace.nasa.gov/constellations/en.

"What Does It Mean to Be Human?" Smithsonian National Museum of Natural History, updated January 22, 2021. See humanorigins.si.edu/evidence/human-fossils/species/homo-sapiens#.

"What Is the Magician's Oath and Why Is It Important." See DailyHistory. org, dailyhistory.org/What_is_the_Magician%27s_Oath_and_why_ is_it_important.

Whipps, Heather. "How Gunpowder Changed the World." LiveScience, April 6, 2008. See www.livescience.com/7476-gunpowder- changed-world.html.

Wigington, Patti. "A Brief History of Tarot." Learn Religions, June 6, 2018. See www.learnreligions.com/a-brief-history-of-tarot-2562770.

Wilson, Clare. "Anglo-Saxon Remedy Kills Hospital Superbug MRSA." *New Scientist*, March 30, 2015. See www.newscientist.com/article/ dn27263-anglo-saxon-remedy-kills-hospital-superbug-mrsa/#.VR0- zuEpqHQ.

Yarnell, Amanda. "History's Hidden Fire." *Chemical & Engineering News*, January 17, 2005. See cen.acs.org/articles/83/i3/Historys-Hidden- Fire.html.

"Zodiac." *Britannica Kids*. See kids.britannica.com/students/article/ zodiac/604121.

ACKNOWLEDGMENTS

There's a fair amount of magic that goes into making a book but also a lot of work, and I couldn't have written this without all the scientists, magicians, and magical people who shared their time, energy, and ideas with me. Of special note is Cassie Gibbs, who invited me into her home, cheerfully answered my questions, and had me obsessively analyzing any animal that crossed my path. Another huge thank-you goes to Tony Barnhart, whose thoughtful skepticism and true love of magic helped me shape my ideas. And this book would have been a lot less fun without Joe Diamond—how did he do that? In addition, I'd like to thank English teacher Laura Thiebes and science teacher Sarah Woodward, who both gave up their precious summer vacation time to read over the manuscript, make invaluable comments, and save me from some potential embarrassment. My unending gratitude goes to Alicia Lincoln, who infused this book with sparkle and always makes my writing better. Thanks to my literary agent, Laura Nolan, and to the team at Abrams Kids, especially my editor, Howard Reeves, and assistant editor Sara Sproull. I'm thrilled that Rafael Nobre again agreed to lend his artistic talent to this project—after seeing his work on the first two books, there's no one else I'd want as an illustrator. My parents, Louise and Chip, and my sister, Ashley, never quite know what strange project I'll be working on next, and I appreciate their unquestioning support and enthusiasm. Likewise, my husband, Scott—a former anthropologist and a once-and-future Dungeon Master—bubbled over with ideas about magic and was happy to discuss every aspect of this book. And of course, thank you to Kira, Alison, and Beth. As the saying goes, friendship is magic. But, like writing a book, it's also work, and I'm so grateful that we've worked to keep our friendship alive and vibrant for over forty years.

INDEX

Note: Page numbers in *italics* refer to illustrations.